SOME MAKERS OF
AMERICAN LITERATURE

SOME MAKERS OF
AMERICAN LITERATURE

BY

WILLIAM LYON PHELPS

Essay Index Reprint Series

 BOOKS FOR LIBRARIES PRESS
FREEPORT, NEW YORK

First Published 1923
Reprinted 1970

STANDARD BOOK NUMBER:
8369-1477-5

LIBRARY OF CONGRESS CATALOG CARD NUMBER:
70-105033

PRINTED IN THE UNITED STATES OF AMERICA

TO
ERNEST M. HOPKINS
PRESIDENT OF DARTMOUTH COLLEGE

PREFACE

I TAKE this opportunity of expressing to the faculty and alumni of Dartmouth, and to the people of Hanover who attended these lectures, my sincere appreciation of their patience, courtesy, and hospitality.

W. L. P.

YALE UNIVERSITY,
Tuesday, 30 *January* 1923.

CONTENTS

SOME MAKERS OF
AMERICAN LITERATURE

SOME MAKERS OF
AMERICAN LITERATURE

I

THE MAN OF THE WORLD AND THE MAN OF GOD

A DRAMATIC CONTRAST

I DO not know who first called attention to the dramatic contrast between those giant contemporaries, Jonathan Edwards, and Benjamin Franklin. I made it the subject of a public lecture twenty-five years ago, and rather flattered myself on being the first to advertise it. Later, on reading an essay by Leslie Stephen, I found that he had made a passing allusion to it in 1874. As a matter of fact, it is so salient that hundreds of students must have observed it. The latest is the accomplished critic, Carl van Doren, who has placed extracts from both writers cheek-by-jowl in one convenient volume. If the pages of that little book could become self-conscious, there would be civil war within the covers.

These two colonial Americans, taken together, reveal every conspicuous trait in American character. Each had to a high degree what the other had not;

each was the other's complement.   If we could take the best in both, and unite the combination in one person, we should have the ideal American.

They were strictly contemporary.   Jonathan Edwards was born in 1703, and Benjamin Franklin in 1706.   Edwards, however, died in 1758, whilst Franklin lived on until 1790.   The man of the world long survived the man of God.

Although both of these men were born in New England, their intellectual lives were as far asunder as east and west.   Edwards's father and grandfather were clergymen: he was a graduate of Yale: a member of the Yale faculty: a preacher in New York and in Northampton: a missionary to the Indians, not in Oklahoma, but in Massachusetts: and he closed his career as President of Princeton.

At the age of ten, he wrote an essay ridiculing the materialistic conception of the soul.   As a man he spent thirteen hours a day in the acquisition of learning, and his favourite studies were Logic, Philosophy, and Metaphysics—studies that for some reason Milton placed in the curriculum of hell.

Others apart sat on a hill retir'd
In thoughts more elevate, and reason'd high
Of Providence, Foreknowledge, Will and Fate—
Fix'd fate, free will, foreknowledge absolute—
And found no end, in wandering mazes lost.

His Resolutions and his Diary show his constant introspection; in those days everyone wrote resolutions, and everyone kept—a diary. He was burdened with that terrible conviction of sin, which seems the least of all modern worries, but which, in colonial days, was at once the cause of mental anguish and yet of rock-like stability of character. The outward life of Edwards seems tame and uneventful; his inner life was wildly exciting, a series of astounding adventures. He scaled vertiginous heights; he fell into unspeakable depths. The Slough of Despond alternated with the Delectable Mountains, from which he had glimpses of the glories of the saints of God.

"My support was in contemplations of the heavenly state; as I find in my Diary for May 1, 1723. It was a comfort to think of that state where there is fulness of joy; where reigns heavenly, calm, and delightful love, without alloy; where there are continually the dearest expressions of this love. . . . Where those persons who appear so lovely in this world, will really be inexpressibly more lovely and full of love to us. And how sweetly will the mutual lovers join together to sing the praises of God and the Lamb. . . . I continued much in the same frame, in the general, as when at New-York, till I went to New-Haven, as tutor in the college. . . . After I went to New-Haven I sunk in religion."

We see that Yale was as desperately wicked a place two hundred years ago as all its enemies admit it to be today.

After he had been a member of the Yale Faculty

for a week, he wrote the following melancholy reflections.

"This has been a remarkable week with me, with respect to despondencies, fears, perplexities, multitudes of cares and distractions of thought, being the week I came hither to New-Haven, in order to entrance upon the office of tutor of the college. I have now abundant reason to be convinced of the troublesomeness and perpetual vexation of the world."

He was, perhaps, with all his learning and consecration, not an ideal teacher for Freshmen: and it is possible that they added to his discomfort. Yet it would be interesting, merely in order to supplement his own diary, if we could have before us the intimate journal of one of the Freshmen. What they thought of him might be as illuminating as what he thought of them.

Edwards was a true mystic; religion was the master-passion of his life. All our feelings of ecstasy aroused by nature, music, poetry, and painting, found in him one outlet—religion. But he was no dreamer, no passive basker in celestial rays. His intellect was of that extremely rare and highly philosophical order, which refuses to regard life as a riddle, except as a riddle to be solved. He sought and found intellectual satisfaction in his religious emotions. Like a hawk after its quarry, he fiercely hunted and fiercely grasped what few seek and fewer find—perfect consistency in his religious beliefs; and he backed them with the full courage of his convictions. Most of us have to leave some enigmas unsolved, most of us have to permit conflicting ideas to jostle along together in our view of the world as best they may—in order that we may get something done before the night cometh. Not so with Edwards: to him the Divine Order became as clear as geometry. Thus he boldly denied the freedom of the will—a doctrine dear to most Christians—since he could not adjust it to the doctrine of predestination. Now the doctrine of predestination meant that the majority of men, women and children—not bad characters, but the general run of folks we now meet on trolley-cars—were moving in grooves toward the everlasting fire. Edwards was both gentle and affectionate in human relations; he would never inflict needless pain on anyone; but as an illustration of how logic can triumph over feeling, let us remember that this kindly man not only swallowed the hideous dogma, but declared that it was palatable. "The doctrine has very often appeared exceeding pleasant, bright and sweet."

The sermons of Edwards, while not eloquent like those of Jeremy Taylor or of Phillips Brooks, had the quiet eloquence of "deeply felt thought." In Mommsen's magnificent *History of Rome,* he compares the eloquence of Cicero to that of Curio, the brilliant lieutenant of Cæsar: he says that the eloquence of Cicero was the eloquence of "rounded periods," whereas that of Curio was, like his master's, the eloquence of "deeply felt thought." In the pulpit Edwards was calm; his manner was glacial: he used simple language; he seldom raised his voice or made a gesture. He described the torments of the damned not in a sensational or melodramatic manner, but as if he were explaining a mathematical demonstration. This composure was tenfold more impressive than if he had screamed, because his dreadful words had behind them the weight of sincerity; they seemed for the moment to be the inescapable truth. Sometimes we see a public speaker excited, while his audience is tranquil; it was the other way when Edwards spoke. He was composed: the audience were in a frenzy.

In describing the destination not of villains, but of the vast majority of respectable citizens, he made it as clear as infinity can be made clear to the finite mind:

"It is everlasting wrath. It would be dreadful to suffer this fierceness and wrath of Almighty God one moment; but you must suffer it to all eternity; there will be no end to this exquisite, horrible misery; when you look forward, you shall see a long forever, a boundless duration, before you, which will swallow up your thoughts and amaze your soul; and you will absolutely despair of ever having any deliverance, any end, any mitigation, any rest at all; you will know certainly that you must wear out long ages, millions and millions of ages, in wrestling and conflicting with this almighty merciless vengeance; and then when you have so done, when so many ages have actually been spent by you in this manner, you will know that all is but a point

to what remains.   So that your punishment will indeed be infinite. . . . If we knew that there was
one person, and but one, in the whole congregation,
that was to be the subject of this misery, what an
awful thing it would be to think of!   If we knew
who it was, what an awful sight would it be to see
such a person!   How might all the rest of the
congregation lift up a lamentable and bitter cry over
him!   But alas!   Instead of one, how many is it
likely will remember this discourse in hell.   And
it would be a wonder if some that are now present
should not be in hell in a very short time, before
this year is out.   And it would be no wonder if
some persons, that now sit here in some seats of
this meeting-house in health, and quiet, and secure,
should be there before tomorrow morning."

If anyone had attempted to turn his dogmas
against himself, and suggested that if men were
predestined to be damned, it was superfluous to
preach to them, I suppose he would have answered
that he could no more help himself than change
their fate: for he was predestined to preach these
very words.   There is no escape from a consistent
logician.

Edwards has often been attacked for delivering
this terrible discourse: personally I admire his courage as much as I admire his mastery of language.
He evidently believed exactly what he said; and I
cannot withhold admiration from those who say
what they really think.   He accepted the consequences of his thought.

It is interesting to observe that when the above extract is read to a modern audience, it arouses laughter. No one laughed when Edwards pronounced it. The reason for the change of effect is that whereas nowadays many people do not seem sure of heaven, everyone seems cocksure that he is not going to hell.

With such beliefs as Edwards held, his sermons, writings, and conduct were logical, natural, and healthy. Intolerance itself often springs from burning conviction; and public opinion today is no more tolerant in some matters than it was centuries ago. We pride ourselves on freedom of thought, on a large tolerance; but the real reason why persons are not persecuted for heresy in religion is chiefly because the public does not believe today that religious scepticism is dangerous to the State. It is not the growth of mercy, still less of charity, but the weakening of conviction, that is the cause of what mental freedom we enjoy. In America, persons are (1923) burned at the stake just as they were in Queen Mary's day; we are not really more civilised. It is the State that has always been supreme. In former days, to be unorthodox was perilous, for loss of office, loss of liberty, loss of life might be the penalty; those who attacked religion were believed to be dangerous citizens. Today it would be difficult to dismiss a public-school teacher because she said she was a religious agnostic; there would be a tremendous clamour, and people would shout that thought must be free; but suppose she says that she does not believe in the government of the country? Is thought free? Has it ever been free? And in the old days when religious heresy was perilous, was it not perilous because at bottom it was believed to be political heresy—quite unpardonable still?

Jonathan Edwards believed in hell-fire, and felt it to be just as clearly his duty to warn people of their danger as any stranger today would warn another if his house were on fire, or if he did not see an approaching train. Some shallow objectors have declared that neither Edwards nor any one else ever really believed in hell, because if they knew millions were suffering such torment, they themselves could neither eat nor sleep, much less laugh and play. But today, although we know at this very moment thousands are dying by famine and tortured by disease in Russia, we do not permit the certain knowledge of that fact to interfere with our programme of business and golf. That way madness lies: we know it, and Edwards knew it, only he ran the chance rather than have people remain in indifference. He was as determined that citizens should not forget hell as your modern social reformer is determined that they shall not forget poverty and disease. I honour him for it.

His sermons were well-known in England. In the *London Magazine*, for June, 1774, I find this notice: "The Justice of God in the Damnation of a Sinner. By the Rev. Jonathan Edwards, M. A., late President of New Jersey College &c. Revised

and Corrected by C. Decoetlogon, M. A. Good
sound Calvinism: imported from America for the
use of the Lock-Chapel."

In his religious meditations, he was by no means
always dwelling within the shadow of his creed.
He had vast depths of saintly tenderness, which are
occasionally revealed in lyrical passages that sound
like "harps in the air."

"Holiness, as I then wrote down some of my
contemplations on it, appeared to me to be of a
sweet, pleasant, charming, serene, calm nature;
which brought an inexpressible purity, brightness,
peacefulness, and ravishment to the soul. In other
words, that it made the soul like a field or garden
of God, with all manner of pleasant flowers; enjoy-
ing a sweet calm and the gently vivifying beams of
the sun. The soul of a true Christian, as I then
wrote my meditations, appeared like such a little
white flower as we see in the spring of the year;
low and humble on the ground, opening its bosom
to receive the pleasant beams of the sun's glory;
rejoicing, as it were, in a calm rapture; diffusing
around a sweet fragrancy; standing peacefully and
lovingly in the midst of other flowers round about;
all in like manner opening their bosoms to drink
in the light of the sun. There was no part of
creature-holiness that I had so great a sense of its
loveliness as humility, brokenness of heart, and
poverty of spirit; and there was nothing that I so
earnestly longed for. My heart panted after this
—to lie low before God, as in the dust; that I might

be nothing, and that God might be all; that I might become as a little child."

Although he was obsessed by divine thoughts, he fell in love with a girl like any other man. Perhaps he would have said that there is no such distinction as that commonly made between sacred and profane love; perhaps all true love to him was sacred. At all events, he was a passionate lover. When he was twenty-two, he wrote on the fly-leaf of a book the following words:

"They say there is a young lady in New-Haven who is beloved of that Great Being, who made and rules the world, and that there are certain seasons in which this Great Being, in some way or other invisible, comes to her and fills her mind with exceeding sweet delight, and that she hardly cares for anything, except to meditate on him—that she expects after a while to be received up where he is, to be raised up out of the world and caught up into heaven; being assured that he loves her too well to let her remain at a distance from him always. There she is to dwell with him, and to be ravished with his love and delight forever. Therefore, if you present all the world before her, with the richest of its treasures, she disregards and cares not for it, and is unmindful of any pain or affliction. She has a strange sweetness in her mind and singular purity in her affections; is most just and conscientious in all her conduct; and you could not persuade her to do anything wrong or sinful, if you would give her all the world, lest she should offend this Great Being. She is of a wonderful sweetness, calmness and universal benevolence of mind; especially after this great God has manifested himself to her mind. She will sometimes go about from place to place, singing sweetly; and seems to be always full of joy and pleasure; and no one knows for what. She loves to be alone, walking in the fields and groves, and seems to have some one invisible always conversing with her."

The man who wrote that passage was fathoms deep in love.

Jonathan Edwards was a great man; he had genius, all of which he used in the exposition, defense and propagation of what he believed to be God's truth. He was the greatest metaphysician this country ever produced; but sometimes I think he was greatest as an ancestor. In every state of the Union, I meet with lineal descendants of Jonathan Edwards. They seem to be desirable citizens. As an ancestor, he was a conspicuous success; he made only one mistake; he was the grandfather of Aaron Burr, for which perhaps he ought not to be held wholly responsible. Now it is a good thing to have a little Edwards in the blood. I should hardly like to be his son; but to have Edwards diluted through five or six generations, ought to give a tonic quality not undesirable. There are indeed some whom it would conceivably improve.

As we learn the chief facts of interest about the life of Edwards from his own writings, we find the same thing true of Franklin. His *Autobiography* is as cheerfully frank as the diary of Pepys, only instead of being set down in cypher, it was openly addressed to his illegitimate son, William. Later this man became governor of New Jersey, and during the War for Independence was an intense Royalist, which caused his father both grief and disgust.

The gods are just, and of our pleasant vices
Make instruments to plague us.

William in turn had an illegitimate son, William Temple Franklin, who was Benjamin's literary executor, and as editor of the *Autobiography* inflicted so many surface wounds on that masterpiece that only a small proportion of its readers even today know what its author actually wrote.

In 1771 Franklin began writing the book at the pleasant town of Twyford, in England; in 1784 he continued its composition at Passy; in 1788 he took it up again at Philadelphia; and in 1789 added a few pages.

The publication of the *Autobiography* is as romantic in its vicissitudes as any of the events it describes. Franklin died in 1790; in 1791 the first edition appeared at Paris, in the French language. This was apparently a surreptitious affair, and how the publisher got hold of the manuscript we do not know. In 1793 two English editions appeared in England, but they were translations of the French version. It was not until 1817, that the *Autobiography,* supposedly as written by Franklin, was published in English under the editorship of William Temple Franklin. He was an ideally bad editor; his first step was to exchange his grandfather's original manuscript with a Frenchman, who owned a transcript which looked cleaner; not content with printing from a copy, when he owned the original, he made more than twelve hundred changes in the text, mostly in the direction of what he considered elegance. One illustration of his methods will suffice. When Franklin described how Governor Keith came to Keimer's printing-office, not to see the proprietor, but the boy, Keimer was so amazed, that according to Franklin, "he stared like a pig poisoned." William Temple evidently thought this a vulgar expression, and changed the homely phrase to "Keimer stared with astonishment."

It was not until 1868, nearly one hundred years after the first part was written, that the *Autobiography* was published from the original manuscript. We owe this immense and permanent contribution to John Bigelow, who was United States Minister to France in 1865. He felt certain that the manuscript must be "somewhere in France," and after innumerable difficulties, involving first class detective work, and the expenditure of large sums of money, he found the precious manuscript in the possession of a French family, bought it and published it for the first time in 1868 exactly as it was written in Benjamin's hand.

Even today there are far more copies in circulation of William Temple's manipulation than of the authentic book; it is important to remember therefore that only Bigelow's edition is correct. Those who are interested in the discovery of the manuscript should read John Bigelow's history of its adventures.

The *Autobiography* has an ineffable charm—it is impossible to imagine any future time when it will not be read with delight. What is the secret of its charm? We are listening to an old man talking. To converse with an old man, who has travelled much, seen much, pondered much—this is one of the keenest pleasures in life. This is the ideal combination of instruction and entertainment. One gets wisdom at the source. You will remember the wonderful conversation between Socrates and the old man at the beginning of Plato's *Republic;* how Socrates asked him if he feared death, if he regretted the loss of youthful pleasures, and what the clear-headed Sage replied to those enquiries.

One thing is especially impressive—in the early paragraphs of the *Autobiography* Franklin says that he would gladly live his life over again. He first makes the proviso, that he shall have the same opportunities to correct mistakes in the repetition that an author has in the second edition of a book. Anyone, I suppose, would jump at that. But he goes on to say, that even if that opportunity were denied, he would still accept the offer. I remember, years ago, in reading Julian Hawthorne's novel, *Archibald Malmaison,* he remarked in the Introduction that no civilised man had ever been found who would be willing to live his life over again. He overlooked Franklin—for whatever Franklin was, he was civilised, far more so than most of the inhabitants of earth in the twentieth century. His declaration prepares us for the calm cheerfulness with which he looked out on the world.

Though a man of wide experience, he was never pessimistic, petulant, or cynical; never nervous or hysterical; always hopeful about the future, and not for a moment afraid of the younger generation knocking at the door. The familiar quarrel between old and young—the prevalent belief in every period of history among the mature that the boys and girls are lacking in morality, earnestness, and the sense of responsibility—was not felt by Franklin. He was quite willing to leave the problems of the future to those who would have to face them.

The charm of the book does not lie mainly in the incidents, though they are sufficiently interesting; the charm lies in Franklin's personality. Wholly apart from his genius, versatility, force, and tact, there was a peculiar personal charm about the man, to which all his acquaintances in Europe and America gave abundant testimony. He was to the highest degree centripetal. He was not an orator, but I suppose there never has lived a more effective committee-man. He was forever trying, usually with success, to persuade a little group to do exactly what he wished. He spent much of his life talking, with momentous consequences to history. And although he spent so many hours in conversation, he never seems to have bored anybody. Imagine a man of whom these four words could truthfully be placed on his tomb—HE NEVER BORED ANYBODY. That epitaph alone would constitute a claim to a prominent position in the celestial choir.

He seems to have been able to say exactly the right word at the opportune moment—apples of gold in pictures of silver. I remember many years ago, when we were visiting some friends in Detroit, and had stayed with them three days, I told them that I thought we must return to New York that afternoon. In the manner of American hospitality, they besought us to remain with them longer; and while we were pleasantly arguing about it, I happened to pick up and open absently a little book that lay near me; I was not even aware of what particular book it was. Now it happened to be *Poor Richard's Almanac*, and just as I had said, "You know we have been here three days," my eyes fell on this passage: "Fish and visitors stink in three days." We left for New York that afternoon.

In reading the *Autobiography*, however, even the most practical and callous mind must observe one limitation in the temperament of the author—a lack of spirituality, with all that the word implies; loftiness of thought, ideality, mysticism, introspection, mental despondency. In Jonathan Edwards this quality was supreme. The attitude of both men toward the study of metaphysics is amusing by contrast. It was the favourite study of Edwards, but after giving it a trial, Franklin remarked, "The great uncertainty I found in metaphysical reasonings disgusted me, and I quitted that kind of reading and study for others more satisfactory."

The Resolutions which each man wrote out clearly betray the sharp opposition in their mental attitudes. This will appear at a glance.

From JONATHAN EDWARDS

"Being sensible that I am unable to do anything without God's help, I do humbly entreat him by his grace, to enable me to keep these Resolutions, so far as they are agreeable to his will, for Christ's sake.

"1. Resolved, That *I will do whatsoever* I think to be most to the glory of God and my own good, profit and pleasure, in the whole . . . without any consideration of the time, whether now, or never so many myriads of ages hence.

"8. Resolved, To act, in all respects, both speaking and doing, as if nobody had been so vile as I, and as if I had committed the same sins, or had the same infirmities or failings as others; and that I will let the knowledge of their failings promote nothing but shame in myself. . . .

"9. Resolved, To think much, on all occasions, of my own dying, and of the common circumstances which attend death.

"38. Resolved, Never to utter anything that is sportive, or matter of laughter, on a Lord's day.

"43. Resolved, Never henceforward, till I die, to act as if I were any way my own, but entirely and altogether God's. . . .

"65. Resolved, Very much to exercise myself in this, all my life long, viz. With the greatest openness, of which I am capable, to declare my ways to

God, and lay open my soul to him, all my sins, temptations, difficulties, sorrows, fears, hopes, desires, and every thing, and every circumstance, according to Dr. Manton's Sermon on the 119th Psalm."

From BENJAMIN FRANKLIN

"1. Temperance.   Eat not to dullness: drink not to elevation.

"5. Frugality.   Make no expense but to do good to others or yourself; i. e., waste nothing.

"9. Moderation.   Avoid extreams: forbear resenting injuries so much as you think they deserve.

"11. Tranquillity.   Be not disturbed at trifles, or at accidents common or unavoidable.

"13. Humility.   Imitate Jesus and Socrates."

It is the emphasis that is so different.   Edwards is thinking of his duty to God, and of the fact of death, and of the next world.   Franklin is thinking of his duty to himself and his neighbours, and of today and tomorrow.   Edwards would say, "Become a Christian, for you might die tonight." Franklin would say, "Become a Christian, in order that you may live wisely tomorrow."   Even where their resolutions are superficially similar, as they are oftener than one might suppose, the emphasis is different.   With Franklin's first resolution, compare the fortieth by Edwards: "To enquire every night, before I go to bed, whether I have acted in the best way I possibly could, with respect to eating and drinking."   Franklin wished to make his bodily machine as effective as possible; Edwards wished to let nothing get between him and the grace of God.

What an enormous increase in our happiness, in our peace of mind, and in our ability to do the day's work would come to pass if we could all live up to Franklin's resolution on Tranquillity! and yet there is not a single person who reads these words, including the man who is writing them, who will be able to keep this Resolution one week. I believe Franklin kept it.

Edwards was a mystic—heaven and hell were clearer to his vision than brooks and meadows; Franklin was a child of this world, a *Weltkind*. Edwards would lie awake all night, thinking of some sin he had imagined himself guilty of committing; Franklin, after committing some gross sin, would write in his journal, "Another erratum," and calmly proceed with the day's work. Edwards looked at the sky, in an agony of prayer and supplication; Franklin, looking in the same direction, tranquilly bottled up the lightning for practical purposes.

It is an interesting query, how far could either have done the other's work? Had Franklin given his powerful mind to metaphysics, he might have written a standard book on Pragmatism, after the later fashion of William James; and it is certain that Edwards, with his acute intellect and his all but divine patience, could have made important discoveries in science. Forty years ago, Professor Henry A. Beers, in his little book on American literature, said of Edwards, "Even as a school-boy and a college student he had made deep guesses in physics as well as metaphysics, and he had early anticipated Berkeley in denying the existence of matter." But Franklin abandoned metaphysics, because it led to no practical results; and Edwards gave up science, as he gave up everything that did not directly minister to salvation.

It would be a great error to suppose that Franklin was not a religious man. He began every day with prayer and he ardently believed in Divine Providence—he believed that God loved him, and that his own life had been divinely guided. He was a practical Christian, reaching the goal not through dogma or conversion, but by the gateway of reason. He firmly believed in the future life. Ezra Stiles, President of Yale College, and be it remembered that Yale was the first institution in the world to give Franklin an honourary degree, wrote him a direct question as to his attitude toward Jesus of Nazareth, and Franklin did not evade the interrogation. This remarkable correspondence took place only a few weeks before Franklin's death, and as it seems not to be so widely known as it ought to be, it cannot be impertinent to quote from it here.

On 28 January 1790, Stiles wrote to Franklin.

"SIR,—We have lately received Governor Yale's portrait from his family. . . . I have also long wished that we might be honoured with that of Dr. Franklin. . . . We wish to be possessed of the durable resemblance of the American Patriot and Philosopher. You have merited and received all the honours of the republic of letters; and are going to a world, where all sublunary glories will be lost in the glories of immortality. Should you shine throughout the intellectual and stellary universe, with the eminence and distinguished lustre, with which you have appeared in this little detached part of the creation, you would be, what I most fervently wish to you, Sir, whatever may be my fate in eternity. . . .

"You know, Sir, that I am a Christian, and would to Heaven all others were such as I am, except my imperfections and deficiencies of moral character. As much as I know of Dr. Franklin, I have not an idea of his religious sentiments. I wish to know the opinion of my venerable friend concerning Jesus of Nazareth. He will not impute this to impertinence or improper curiosity, in one, who for so many years has continued to love, estimate, and reverence his abilities and literary character, with an ardour and affection bordering on adoration. If I have said too much, let the request be blotted out, and be no more; and yet I shall never cease to wish you that happy immortality, which I believe Jesus alone has purchased for the virtuous and truly good of every religious denomination in Christendom, and for those of every age, nation, and mythology, who reverence the Deity, are filled with integrity, righteousness, and benevolence. Wishing you every blessing, I am, dear Sir, your most obedient servant,

"EZRA STILES."

Franklin replied,

"I received your kind letter of January 28th,
and . . . am however too much obliged to Yale
College, the first learned society that took notice
of me and adorned me with its honours, to refuse
a request that comes from it through so esteemed
a friend. . . . You have an excellent artist lately
arrived. If he will undertake to make one for you,
I shall cheerfully pay the expense; but he must not
delay setting about it, or I may slip through his
fingers, for I am now in my eighty-fifth year, and
very infirm.

"You desire to know something of my religion.
It is the first time I have been questioned upon it
But I cannot take your curiosity amiss, and shall
endeavour in a few words to gratify it. Here is
my creed. I believe in one God, the creator of the
universe. That he governs it by his Providence.
That he ought to be worshipped. That the most
acceptable service we render to him is doing good
to his other children. That the soul of man is
immortal, and will be treated with justice in another life respecting its conduct in this. These I
take to be the fundamental points in all sound religion, and I regard them as you do in whatever sect
I meet with them.

"As to Jesus of Nazareth, my opinion of whom
you particularly desire, I think his system of morals
and his religion, as he left them to us, the best the
world ever saw or is like to see; but I apprehend
it has received various corrupting changes, and I

have, with most of the present Dissenters in England, some doubts as to his Divinity; though it is a question I do not dogmatize upon, having never studied it, and think it needless to busy myself with it now, when I expect soon an opportunity of knowing the truth with less trouble. . . .

"I shall only add, respecting myself, that, having experienced the goodness of that Being, in conducting me prosperously through a long life, I have no doubt of its continuance in the next, though without the smallest conceit of meriting such goodness. . . .

"I confide, that you will not expose me to criticisms and censures by publishing any part of this communication to you. I have let others enjoy their religious sentiments without reflecting on them for those that appeared to me unsupportable or even absurd. All sects here, and we have a great variety, have experienced my good will in assisting them with subscriptions for the building their new places of worship; and, as I have never opposed any of their doctrines, I hope to go out of the world in peace with them all."

As Edwards anticipated Berkeley in metaphysics, Franklin anticipated the theology of Matthew Arnold, and in definition actually surpassed in concision that master of English style. Matthew Arnold explained God as "A Power, not ourselves, that works for righteousness." Benjamin Franklin expressed the same idea in two words—*Powerful Goodness*.

The keynote to Franklin's temperament is the word *Curiosity*, used, not in its village connotation, but in its highest and widest import. Boundless, unquenchable curiosity. Of reverence he had little; he was hampered by no tradition or convention; he must enquire into everything for himself. It was this quality which produced his discoveries in Electricity, which alone would have made him immortal. As a boy, I supposed the finding of Electricity was his sole occupation; whenever I thought of Franklin, I saw a picture of a portly man in knee-breeches, with a benevolent expression on his countenance, standing in the 1ain and flying a kite Later, I knew that his discovery of electricity was only a half-holiday in his busy life. He invented the Franklin stove, still the best open stove in the world. It was intolerable to his mind that an implement which produced the blessing of heat should also contribute the curse of smoke. ' He invented the new street-lamps, making them shine all night by the simple device of an air-draught; he originated the street-cleaning department, the fire-department, the Philadelphia public library, the *Saturday Evening Post,* and the University of Pennsylvania. He invented the bi-focal eyeglasses—one of the greatest of blessings—to fit his own needs. At Paris he frequently dined out where there were beautiful women in the company. Like all sensible men, he was fond of good food, and fond of looking at lovely women. He declared it to be important to see your food before you put it into your mouth; but he also wished to see the faces of the guests that decorated the table. It was inconvenient to put on one pair of spectacles to eat, and another pair every time anybody spoke to him.   He therefore hit upon the device of having the upper part of his glasses consist of one lens, and the lower of another, which proved in practice, like nearly everything he thought of, eminently satisfactory.   To Franklin everything he saw, from a thunderstorm to a lamp-post, was a problem to be solved, the solution to be for the additional security and comfort of mankind.

Franklin has often been attacked for what has been called his parsimony.   I read somewhere that Jefferson Davis denounced him as "the incarnation of the peddling, tuppenny Yankee."   Was he mean? The answer to this is his own life.   He never held up riches as a goal.   Liberty and independence and the power of doing good can be obtained through money.   If your expenses are greater than your income, he said, then you are some one's slave, and perhaps a burden to the whole community.   If your income exceed your expenses, no matter by how small a margin, then you are free and can look everyone in the face.   If God loves a cheerful giver, He must have loved Franklin.   He went about doing good, and we cannot doubt that in this occupation he found his highest happiness.   Most of us, even when we give, give reluctantly, often with painful effort; Franklin gave not only voluntarily, but eagerly.   No man ever was more wisely generous. He formed the habit of doing good every day of his life.   In a long letter sent to him about various matters from an acquaintance, the writer mentioned incidentally that his eyes were troubling him.   I dare say that if the average person received such a letter, he would either make no comment on that diseasement, or would content himself by an expression of vague hope. Franklin sent the man, who had asked for nothing, a number of pairs of glasses, saying that if his eyes were troubling him, it was probably owing to his not having the proper spectacles. He advised him to try them all, use the pair that relieved him, keep the stronger ones for use as he advanced in years, and give the weaker ones away to some younger person who might need them.

In public affairs he was equally generous. I suppose that every state in the Union has a town named after him. Some one in Franklin, Massachusetts, informed him of the honour done him there, and requested a donation of money to put a bell in the church-tower. Franklin sent the money, but suggested that instead of a bell, they buy a library; "for I have always preferred sense to sound." Having some curiosity to know whether this library existed, and how large it was, I received a letter from Mrs. H. A. Smith, giving the complete catalogue of books in the original Franklin library, founded there in 1786. There were 116 books in the original library, showing that the gift of money must have been considerable; and today there remain 86.

Franklin never regarded himself as a man of letters, and had apparently no ambition whatever for literary reputation. In his youth, Addison's *Spectator* was in the flush of its early fame, and he originally attempted to found his style on Addison, so that he might be able to express himself clearly; and indeed his set pieces instantly remind one of the *Spectator*. But the beauty of the *Autobiography* is not the beauty of Addison—its stylistic charm is in its simplicity. Although Franklin did not pretend to be a literary man, and founded no school of letters, he accomplished one thing with his pen that seems miraculous—he made the most ephemeral form of writing live forever; he gave immortality to an Almanac!

Franklin has often been called the Typical American; but in one important aspect he was not typical at all. He was without the typical national nervousness. Nearly every educated American has either had nervous prostration, is having it now, or is just about to have it. The malady is so familiar that it is frequently diagnosed as Americanitis. It is difficult to imagine Franklin suffering with "nerves." One reason was that he was too steadily busy to think much about himself, but that does not altogether explain his happy immunity. He possessed the extraordinary faculty of being able at any moment to shift the gear of his mind; so that while doing one thing he was not thinking of another; never trying to solve tomorrow's problems while occupied with those of today; not having anxiety as a nocturnal bedfellow. He had the temper of a stage Dutchman. It was his tranquil way of mind that enabled him to turn the full power of his brain on any selected object. His equable judgment is particularly well shown in the manner of regarding those who had injured him. Most of us

cannot stand outside the circle of our own grievances. If some one has treated us ill, it is difficult
for us to judge that person's ability and accomplishments with complete aloofness. Not so Franklin.
The cruel trick played on him by Governor Keith
might have destroyed a less hardy personality. The
boy Franklin in England, relying on Keith's patronage, found that he had been sent on a fool's errand;
there he stood, in a strange land, many weeks away
from home, with no money and no friends. Instead
of committing suicide, he sought work. As one
walks along a London street today, and sees the
tablet on a certain building, commemorating the fact
that Benjamin Franklin once lodged there, one cannot repress a thrill, remembering that a homeless
waif eventually made such an impression as to add
by his mere presence imperishable glory to the
metropolis of the world.

In the *Autobiography,* Franklin mentions the
treachery shown to him by Keith, and then adds,
"Several of our best laws were of his planning and
passed during his administration." No remark
could more clearly display magnificent intellectual
health; in such a nature there was no room for the
poison of malice.

Perhaps there never was a man who combined to
so high a degree Efficiency and Charm. The very
word efficiency has grown repulsive to many original
minds, for it seems to connote merely mechanical
force. Now Franklin had so much efficiency that
some was left over for his family; his grand-niece
used to say her morning prayers coming down the

stair-case, that no time might be wasted. Yet, combined with his tireless activity, his mind was so interesting as to nullify, in his instance, an apology for idlers. No graceless vagabond ever had more charm. Your tremendously efficient man is sometimes rather lacking in a sense of humour; Franklin was one of the world's great humourists.

Like his contemporary, Goethe, whom he resembles in so many ways—the chief difference being that Goethe was one of the best, and Franklin one of the worst of poets—he was astonishingly *modern* in his point of view. We shall probably have to advance for centuries before we catch up with the mind of Goethe or of Franklin. His modernity was so noticeable that if he could now return to earth, it would only be a week or two before he would feel completely at home. He advocated daylight-saving, which was not adopted in the United States until 1918, and later voted down by Congress. He ardently urged that all children should be taught to write with either hand; this is one of the rarest accomplishments on earth, and yet it ought to be universal, and could be. He called attention to the enormous number of people who earn their living by the right hand; when this becomes disabled, they are out of work, and have to be supported. How easily such a loss could be prevented! In the year 1914, this matter was seriously discussed in the English schools, and might have been adopted, had not the war interfered. But it was in his attitude toward the folly and tragedy of war that Franklin was so far ahead of his and of our time. He said,

"All wars are follies, very expensive, and very mis-
chievous ones. When will mankind be convinced
of this, and agree to settle their differences by arbi-
tration?" When indeed? Theoretically, he was
an extreme pacifist. After the War for Independence, although his side had been victorious, he
said, "There never was a good war or a bad peace."
On another occasion, he remarked that it would be
better for nations to settle their differences by toss-
ing a coin, rather than by resorting to war. He
wished that in time of war merchant ships, both neutral and those belonging to belligerents, should not
be destroyed, but that trade should progress freely.
His practical worldly wisdom, however, is shown
in the fact that he was never a slave to theory, not
even to his own. After trying for years to avert
war with England, using every resource at his com-
mand, he recognised the fact of war when it came.
He fought as efficiently as he had tried to prevent
fighting. He was worth to the American cause more
than a large army. He fought with all his might
every moment from the declaration of war to
the declaration of peace, in order to bring the
tragedy as soon as possible to a close.

Up to the actual outbreak of the war, England
had no more loyal or devoted friend than Franklin;
during the progress of the conflict, England had no
more formidable or dangerous foe.

It is often said that his life shows what can be
accomplished by Industry. Such a statement is
very wide of the mark. Franklin was a man of
genius; and his career can be explained, if explained

at all, only by the mystery of genius. No one knows what genius is, but its presence is manifest. It cannot be explained by heredity. What shall we say of Keats, whose father was a livery-stable keeper? and in that stable the son found the only horse who was not there—Pegasus. What of Burns, whom J. M. Barrie calls the greatest of all Scots? his father was a peasant. What of Carlyle, whose father was an ignorant stone mason? Consider Franklin: he was one of seventeen children, and he did not occupy a conspicuous place in the assembly. He was neither youngest nor oldest, but obscurely placed third from the last. Neither his father nor his mother, nor a single one of his brothers or sisters, ever displayed the slightest trace of genius. The wind bloweth where it listeth: what divine breath hovered over that crowded Boston nest, and inspired Benjamin? Matthew Arnold said he was the greatest of all Americans; and it would be difficult indeed to name a greater. He stood the test of comparison with the foremost men of his time. "Seest thou a man diligent in his business? He shall stand before kings." "I have stood before five," he said with humour. He was first in many different ways. This self-educated, homespun American came in England and in France into competition with men who had every advantage that birth, breeding, education, and refinement can give; he never met a diplomat who did not in his heart recognise his superior. He was adored by the leaders of Parisian society. In practical emergencies his judg-

ment was all but infallible. He was a great
scientist when organised science was in its infancy;
his statesmanship was surpassed by that of no contemporary; one of the favourite books of the world
was written by him; he is the only man who signed
the Declaration of Independence, the French Treaty
of Alliance, the Treaty of Peace, and the United
States Constitution. He was the most useful man
in the world; a tower of strength, a multitudinous
blessing. It would be well for the world today if
there were a statesman anywhere who approached
him in ability. If he were only with us, how greatly
he could aid a tumultuous and tormented planet!

If in the future some man should appear, who
should combine the sincere piety, idealism, purity,
and uncompromising morality of Jonathan Edwards,
with the profound wisdom, insight, humour, tact,
and kindliness of Franklin, then we should have the
ideal American. If such men became numerous, we
should have the Millennium.

II

THE SPIRIT OF ROMANCE

JAMES FENIMORE COOPER

COOPER belongs among the world's great Romantics—Scott, Dumas, Victor Hugo, Stevenson, Sienkiewicz. He has survived the arrows of outrageous criticism, and survived what is even more deadly, the crushing bulk of his own work. He brought to the gates of immortality an enormous amount of excess baggage. He himself, however, is on the right side of the gates, though only a small portion of his works have followed him. Just why so careless and hasty a writer has outlived so many meticulous artists, is an interesting question. I shall endeavour to suggest an answer.

Cooper was born in 1789, the year of the French Revolution. This turbulent time was a fitting matrix for the appearance of one of the most independent, fiery, challenging, and combative men in American literature. His life-motto might have been *Venienti Occurrite Morbo;* he was always looking for trouble. He was born in Burlington, New Jersey. I wish that I knew exactly what was in the mind of Dr. Johnson when he wrote, in his *Life of Waller,* "Benjamin, the eldest son, was disinherited, and sent to New Jersey as wanting common understanding." We know that Johnson had no great admiration for Americans, for he remarked, "Sir, they are a race of convicts, and ought to be thankful for anything we allow them short of hanging." But in so general a condemnation, why this special tribute to New Jersey? However this may be, Cooper did not long remain in the vicinity of his natal town. He moved to the lake region of central New York at the age of one.

Cooper entered Yale College in the class of 1806. With one exception, he was the youngest student in the institution. By paying little attention to the curriculum, he received considerable attention from the Faculty; so much indeed, that in his Junior year he was expelled. He was not dissipated, he was insubordinate.

He became by far the most famous man-of-letters who ever attended Yale, but in his case the Faculty may be pardoned for not detecting his genius. The college library owns a silhouette taken of him in his undergraduate days—the profile of a boy in which the chief expression seems to be determination. In the twentieth century, four of his great-grandsons were graduated from Yale. One of them, James Fenimore Cooper, lost his life in the World War, and left behind him a volume of original poems, which have been published under the title *Afterglow.*

Finding the discipline of the college professors too strict, Cooper, in the autumn of 1806, discovered the actual meaning of the word. It was always characteristic of him, that if he found an obstacle which he could not surmount, he immediately sought one more difficult. If he were too tired to climb a hill, he attacked a mountain. He went before the mast on a merchant vessel, and saw London and the Mediterranean. On the first of January 1808, he became a Midshipman in the United States Navy, little dreaming what use he would eventually make of his knowledge and experience.

In 1811 he resigned from the Navy, was married, and found the chief happiness of his life in his home. He soon went back to the old estate at Cooperstown, one of the most beautiful places in America, and which he was to make forever a resort for literary pilgrims. He subsequently lived for a time in Westchester County, the famous "neutral ground" where the scenes in *The Spy* were laid; in 1822 he moved to New York City, and in 1826 went to Europe with his family and remained seven years. From 1833 until his death in 1851 he lived in Cooperstown, now the home of his grandson, James Fenimore Cooper, to whom we owe valuable historical publications dealing with the place, as well as a collection of letters written by the novelist.

The later years of Cooper's life were unfortunately largely occupied in quarrels with various newspapers, against which he frequently brought suits for libel. Even when he won it was a Pyrrhic victory; for the journals naturally used the weapon of ridicule, and Cooper devoted nights and days to fruitless combat, which he might much better have spent in literary composition, or in contemplating

the beauty of his natural surroundings. The echoes
of this inky warfare were heard across the ocean,
and in the journalistic amenities of those happy
years, the *London Times* and *Fraser's Magazine*
bestowed upon Cooper's head a blizzard of epithets
that sounds like a catalogue of a zoological collection. Greeley's *New Yorker* tried to destroy him
with hard words, which merely increased the hitting
power of the designed victim. Cooper always returned to the fray, like the indomitable antagonist
he was; he believed in his heart not only in the
justice of his cause, but that he was performing a
valuable public service. How important, how over-
whelmingly important his "case" seemed to him
then! Today it is forgotten, and the public knows
Cooper only as a novelist. All the time spent on
controversy is wasted; if both parties gain by a
trade, both parties lose by a fight; and it is more
profitable to attack a windmill than a newspaper.

Cooper is more admirable when discussing literature. In 1841 he was asked to contribute to
a new magazine, which was to be both big in size
and remunerative to its contributors. His letter,
which has hitherto not been printed, contains the
following: "I never asked or took a dollar in my
life, for any personal service, except as an officer
in the Navy, and for full grown books. . . . Do
you think size as important in a journal, as quality?
We have so much mediocrity in this country, that,
excuse me for saying it, I think distinction might
better now be sought in excellence."

Cooper was so prolific that in writing the above

letter he may have had himself in mind. He was the author of over thirty novels, many books of travel, and masses of polemics.

The decade from 1821 to 1831 was the most fruitful. These were his happiest years; he was famous and the clouds of hostility had not yet obscured the sky. He was welcomed everywhere in Europe as a distinguished novelist, and his letters written abroad, first published by his grandson in 1922, reveal his cheerful activities in composition and his literary friendships. Writing to his wife from Genoa in 1829, he must have thought of the contrast between his first visit to the Mediterranean as a common seaman, and his second visit as a famous man. He, however, looked back to those early days with something of the pleasure that Mark Twain enjoyed in his recollections of the Mississippi. Cooper wrote:

"I am at the Croix de Malta, which looks directly on the harbour. I can scarcely describe to you the pleasure I feel in seeing ships, hearing the cries of seamen, a race everywhere so much alike, and in smelling all the odours of the trade. Yesterday I did the harbour thoroughly, by land and water, floating in the Mediterranean again, after an interval of twenty-one years, with a delight like that of a schoolboy, broke out of his bounds."

Among the authors he met in Paris, was Sir Walter Scott. In a letter to her sister, Mrs. Cooper thus describes him:

"He was with us several times, and treated Mr.
Cooper, like a Son or Younger Brother, in the
same vocation—He is a Giant in form, as He is
one in Literature—to you who are craniologists, I
must mention that his head, is uncommonly high,
and narrow,—he is very gray—and has a fine florid,
healthy appearance—he talks a great deal and
quotes old Ballads, and Shakespeare, very happily
& pleasantly—and to this I will add that He has
quite a rustic appearance—and still further, but this
is for your private ear alone—that He put me in
mind of one of our country Presbyterian Parsons—
altogether—He looks like a Man of powerful mind
—kind and amiable, as if He liked fun—and withal
very countrified."

It was natural that Cooper should have been frequently called the American Scott; equally natural
that he should have resented the appellation.
Writers are perhaps more jealous of their personality even than the average run of mankind. In a
letter to a man who had published an encomium on
his novels, Cooper wrote from Paris, 21 May 1831,
(first printed in 1922):

"For your good opinion, it is my business to
thank you. I shall not do this much however, without raising a point of difference between us. In
a note you call me the 'rival of Sir Walter Scott.'
Now the idea of rivalry with him never crossed my
brain. I have always spoken, written and thought
of Sir Walter Scott (as a writer) just as I should

think and speak of Shakespeare—with high admiration of his talent, but with no silly reserve, as if I thought my own position rendered it necessary that I should use more delicacy than other men. . . . If there is a term that gives me more disgust than any other, it is to be called, as some on the continent advertise me, the 'American Walter Scott.' It is offensive to a gentleman to be nicknamed at all, and there is a pretension in the title, which offends me more than all the abusive reviews that ever were written."

From 1821 to 1831 he was in the vein. During the years immediately preceding his visit to Europe in 1826, and during his residence abroad, he composed with astonishing ease. In 1821 appeared *The Spy*, in 1823 *The Pioneers* and *The Pilot* (both germinal works), in 1825 *Lionel Lincoln*, in 1826 *The Last of the Mohicans*, in 1827 *The Prairie*, and in 1828 *The Red Rover*. Few authors can show so splendid an output in so short a time. And before he returned to America in 1833, he had written *The Water Witch, The Bravo, The Wept of Wish-ton-Wish* and *The Heidenmauer*. He always regarded *The Bravo* as one of his best books.

Long before the era of the best-sellers, it is worth remembering that on the day when *The Pioneers* was published, 3500 copies were sold before noon.

The beginning of his literary career is in sharp contrast to that of Stevenson, which may partly account for their difference in style. Cooper served no apprenticeship to any author, made no prolonged study of the art of composition, and had reached the age of thirty without having apparently any literary ambition. One day he was reading aloud to his wife a novel of English society, and he made the comment that nine out of ten readers make on most books: "I believe I could write a better story myself." Mrs. Cooper challenged him to try; and he, who had never from boyhood refused a "dare," immediately began writing a novel that so far as I can discover—for I have no intention of reading it —deserves among all books the booby prize. *Precaution* is not only admitted to be hopelessly bad in structure and in characters and in style, but it had the bad luck of being a comedy of typographical errors.

To use the American vernacular, Cooper "broke into" literature; he came over the wall, not through the strait gate. And it is perhaps fortunate that his first novel was so impressingly unimpressive. Had it been a success, he might have triumphantly said, "That's that," and never written again. But he had the dauntless spirit that while it finds in success encouragement, finds in failure glowing inspiration. He made the stumbling-block a stepping-stone. The dates are significant: *Precaution* 1820, *The Spy* 1821. John Jay had told Cooper the story of a spy, which Cooper turned into one of the most successful novels in American literature. Yet neither the public nor the publisher had any hope for this venture. Never were the canons of art more contemptuously defied. The publisher received the sheets as they were written and became alarmed at what seemed to him the probable length of the tale. He wrote remonstratingly to the author who stopped midway in his task, wrote the last chapter, sent it on, told the publisher to have it set up, printed, paged, and numbered, so that he might know for his peace of mind the extreme limit of the book. All this being done, Cooper then wrote just enough to fill the gap.

The Spy scored a prodigious success, and deserved it. The vitality of the story triumphed over its cutaneous blemishes. The death of brave Captain Lawton, and the hanging of the Skinner by the Cow-Boys are narrated by a master's hand. These events are as vivid to me now as when I first saw them in the book nearly fifty years ago.

The figure of The Spy, as a supreme example of patriotism—the sacrifice of one's honour for one's country is rightly regarded as a greater sacrifice than one's life—is forever appealing. It may be sweet to die for your country, but there can be nothing sweet in deliberately giving up your personal honour and your good name. The poignancy of the Spy's tragedy as shown by Cooper was set forth again by Augustus Thomas in *The Copperhead* with the scenes changed from the War of the Revolution to the War of the Rebellion.

The first two novels of Cooper, one beneath criticism, and the other a masterpiece, sufficiently display his inequalities as a writer. When he portrays the life, manners, and conversation of people in aristocratic society, he is positively bad; when he is on the high seas, or in the vast woods, he is superb.

He cannot make ladies and gentlemen seem real;
but his trappers, his Indians, and his sailors are
magnificently alive. His failure was not the common one, due to ignorance of the material; he was
a gentleman born and bred, and knew how people
behaved in social intercourse. Why then could he
not draw them convincingly?

I think it was because in that field he had no
sympathetic imagination. One must have much
more than knowledge and experience to write good
fiction—if we must choose, creative imagination is
more fruitful than either. In the forest and on
the ocean, he lived with his characters; they were
more real to him than his neighbours; whereas at
his desk he apparently could not see the children of
fashion. They eluded him.

I wonder if all Americans realise the prodigious
and world-wide popularity of Cooper's romances.
Only the other day I was reading a short story by
Chekhov, where in a Russian village two romantic
boys call each other "Montezuma Hawkeye" and
"my Paleface Brother." Russian and Polish children are as familiar with the *Leather-Stocking
Tales* as their American contemporaries. Professor
Lounsbury quotes Morse, the inventor of the elec-
tric telegraph, who wrote, "I have visited, in
Europe, many countries, and what I have asserted
of the fame of Mr. Cooper, I assert from personal
knowledge. In every city of Europe that I visited
the works of Cooper were conspicuously placed in
the windows of every bookshop. They are published as soon as he produces them in thirty-four

different places in Europe. They have been seen by American travellers in the languages of Turkey and Persia, in Constantinople, in Egypt, at Jerusalem, at Ispahan."

One reason why Cooper is translated with such success is because his books, although one hundred per cent American, particularly lend themselves to translation. Unlike most masterpieces, they can be translated without losing anything. We can go still further. As the interest lies in the incidents and in the narration, and as they were written for the most part in a bad English style, every time they were translated they were improved. I feel sure that the French, German, Spanish, Italian, Russian, Polish, Turkish and Japanese children who delight in Cooper hold in their little hands a better book than the original.

At that time English criticism was looked upon as indispensable. If an American wrote a book, he waited with alternate hopes and fears, for the supreme court of British opinion to hand down a decision. Some Americans may still be seen in this expectant attitude. Cooper pretended that his first novel had been written by an Englishman—I sincerely hope his readers believed him. At that time England rather despised American culture, and many cultivated Americans despised their countrymen; which made a decided handicap for any ambitious young author in the United States. Even today it is not difficult to detect a "certain condescension."

Cooper's most patriotic service was outside of

the navy. He did much by his novels to awaken in Europe both admiration and respect for American books. He was naturally called "the American Scott," and with some reason; for he resembles Scott both in his merits and in his defects. The more Cooper advanced his own fortunes, the more he helped his country. We should be grateful to our first important novelist.

Furthermore, of all our early writers, he was most truly and consistently American. This is perhaps more appreciated now than then. He created an American literature out of American materials, a literature which had in it no echoes of Europe. I suppose, after his false start, he was less influenced by foreign authors and foreign subjects than any of his contemporaries. In an estimate of his work, this fact should not be forgotten.

As Cooper wrote *Precaution* in response to a challenge, it was the same motive that was the only begetter of his first sea-story, *The Pilot*. Scott's *Pirate* appeared in 1821, and it formed the topic of table-conversation at a dinner where Cooper happened to be present. Some one expressed surprise that Scott, who was a landsman, could have shown such nautical knowledge. Cooper replied that a professional seaman could have done much better, and he added that a novel, written from a sailor's point of view, would be more interesting. His table-companions vigorously dissented—the details would bore the general reader, and would distress an Old Salt. This was enough for the man who never took a dare; he announced his determination to prove his words, and in 1823 appeared *The Pilot*.

In a later preface, 10 August 1849, Cooper spoke of the origin of the book:

"It is probable a true history of human events would show that a far larger proportion of our acts are the results of sudden impulses and accident, than of that reason of which we so much boast.   However true, or false, this opinion may be in more important matters, it is certainly and strictly correct as relates to the conception and execution of this book. . . . The result of this conversation was a sudden determination to produce a work, which, if it had no other merit, might present truer pictures of the ocean and ships than any that are to be found in the *Pirate*.   To this unpremeditated decision, purely an impulse, is not only the *Pilot* due, but a tolerably numerous school of nautical romances that have succeeded it.

"The author had many misgivings concerning the success of the undertaking, after he had made some progress in the work; the opinions of his different friends being anything but encouraging.   One would declare that the sea could not be made interesting; that it was tame, monotonous, and the less he got of it the better.   The women very generally protested that such a book would have the odour of bilgewater, and that it would give them the *maladie de mer*.   Not a single individual among all those who discussed the merits of the project, within the range of the author's knowledge, either spoke, or

looked, encouragingly.   It is probable that all these
persons anticipated a signal failure."

This extract proves that the book was suddenly
conceived and that its author's object was two-fold:
1. To beat Scott's seamanship.
2. To show that the sea was available for literature.

His success was immediate and striking; and I
think he was more pleased at his triumph over his
sceptical friends than at the addition to his literary
fame.

The Pilot founded a new school in fiction, which
has flourished abundantly.   Smollett had taken his
readers on the sea, but it was not the basis of his
work.   Captain Marryat, Herman Melville, Clark
Russell, Stevenson, and Joseph Conrad have succeeded in making the sea "interesting."   Seventeen
years after *The Pilot,* appeared that imperishable
work, *Two Years Before the Mast,* which resembled
Cooper in its accidental entrance into immortality.

In his preface, Cooper spoke contemptuously of
that part of the human race without whose support
novelists could not live.   Women are just as necessary to novelists as they are to symphony or-
chestras, art galleries, and foreign missions.   If
they withdrew their patronage, writers of fiction,
painters, musicians, and Christian ministers would
starve.

"*The Pilot* could scarcely be a favourite with
females.   The story has little interest for them, nor

was it much heeded by the author of the book, in the progress of his labours.   His aim was to illustrate vessels, not the weaker one, and the ocean, rather than to draw any pictures of sentiment and love.   In this last respect, the book has small claims on the reader's attention, though it is hoped that the story has sufficient interest to relieve the more strictly nautical features of the work."

Possibly he was still angry at what some of the females said at the germinal dinner.

Cooper was correct in his appraisal of the various portions of this novel.   The chapters he enjoyed writing are very fine; the love-stuff he mechanically used for "relief" is no better than he thought it was.

And yet the women in *The Pilot* are as true to life as those in his other books.   Cooper could not draw real women.   A century has passed since he manufactured these females, and they seem much worse to us than to his contemporaries, because the girl-model has so completely changed.   His women are timid, shrinking, and abnormally refined.   As Lounsbury says, "His heroines have a combination of propriety and incapacity."   This may perhaps be partly explained by Cooper's chivalrous, idealising attitude.   He was a virile, fighting man, who looked upon women as attractively frail, weak, and helpless.   In this very book, he declares, "A woman is never so interesting as when she leans on man for support."   That depends.

Cooper should not be exclusively blamed for these insipid puppets.   He was crudely following the ideal of his day; and to see how fashions change with the times, one may read any popular American twentieth-century novel. Describing a "real lady," Cooper said, "On one occasion her little foot moved," although "she had been carefully taught too that even this beautiful portion of the female frame should be quiet and unobtrusive."

At about the same time when Cooper was writing *The Pilot,* Washington Irving published the following:

"Nothing can be more touching than to behold a soft and tender female, who had been all weakness and dependence, and alive to every trivial roughness, while treading the prosperous paths of life, suddenly rising in mental force to be the comforter and support of her husband under misfortune, and abiding, with unshrinking firmness, the bitterest blasts of adversity."

Decorum perhaps was never the real god of women; that form of worship was forced upon them by their conquerors, and they have now become independent.

As Cooper in his later preface practically warned women that there was nothing for them in his book, in his original one he attempted to forestall possible adverse criticism from men by telling them defiantly they were landlubbers and had better not betray their ignorance.

In this novel Cooper does not describe the sea; he takes us thither. We feel the salt mist in our face; the deck slants; we hear the wind in the rigging; we see the white flashes of the breakers precariously near, followed by the reassuring rhythm of the long waves on the open ocean.

In description and in narration he is a master. The pursuit of the whale, so familiar to modern readers in later books, is told by Cooper with thrilling intensity.

In one hundred years, sea-fiction has grown up. The stories of Conrad and Cooper form a fruitful contrast. It is the difference between the subjective and the objective; between profound analysis and running narrative; between a style in which every word has been carefully selected and a style completely lacking in self-consciousness, hastily adapted to the necessary incidents. Cooper saw, remembered, and wrote; Conrad saw, remembered, pondered deeply, and gave us the results of his experiences as coloured by philosophical meditation. The evolution of sea-fiction from Cooper to Conrad is the evolution from the simple and spontaneous, to the complex and self-conscious.

Why does the normal man love stories of the sea? In vain have I tried to analyse my delight in them. I have never sailed a cat-boat alone, much less a yacht; I have never cruised or travelled a long distance in a vessel impelled only by the wind. None of my ancestors, so far as I know, was a sea-faring man. And yet I had rather read novels of the sea than any others; nor do I care how technical they are. I love the moment when finally cargo and crew are aboard, and the ship is tugged toward the harbour's mouth, for I know that soon I shall be out of sight of land, where, in the pages of a book, I am perfectly happy. If I were a millionaire, I would not own a steam yacht, I would have made for me a full-rigged ship, with no auxiliary, and with a party of friends, I would sail around the Horn. After all, I wonder if I should. I have rounded the Horn scores of times with various authors, and millions of times in imagination; perhaps it would not be necessary to take my body there.

Cathedrals on the land and sailing ships on the sea are the most beautiful works of man.

Over and over again I have read Clark Russell's *Wreck of the Grosvenor*, Stevenson's *Treasure Island, Ebb Tide,* and *Wrecker,* Conrad's *Typhoon* and *Nigger of the Narcissus,* Melville's *Moby Dick,* Dana's *Two Years Before the Mast,* and many less distinguished works which give me much the same thrill. In our own times, the stories of Ben Ames Williams and William John Hopkins and Charles Boardman Hawes and Arthur Mason find me a willing victim. All the greater is my gratitude to Fenimore Cooper for proving that the sea could be made "interesting" and thus becoming the ancestor of all these worthies.

How absurd is the criticism that in *The Pilot* the author made John Paul Jones melodramatic! If he had made him anything else, he would have made him altogether unreal. No hero of romance was ever more melodramatic than that extraordinary sailor of fortune, whose life was stranger than fiction.

Despite the excellence of *The Spy, The Red Rover,* and *The Pilot,* Cooper was, is, and probably will continue to be best known by his *Leather-Stocking Tales.* They were published originally in this order: *Pioneers,* 1823; *Mohicans,* 1826; *Prairie,* 1827; *Pathfinder,* 1840; *Deerslayer,* 1841.

It will be observed that the first three books were written within five years; then came an interval of thirteen years, and the last two followed with only a twelvemonth between them. In view of the steady development of the hero's growth and character, and the regular march of incidents, which has caused the whole series to be accurately designated as a drama in five acts, with five different names for leading man, it is surprising that no two of the novels were written in what now seems the natural order. *Deerslayer,* which comes first, was written last: *Mohicans* was written after the *Pioneers, Pathfinder* was written next to the last, *Pioneers* the fourth, was written first, and the series concludes with *Prairie,* which was written third.

Originally Cooper had no intention of expansion; he had not even thought of a "trilogy." After the publication of *The Pioneers,* he happened to make an excursion to Lake George with a party of friends in 1825, and one of his companions suggested that here was the very scene for a romance. The remark was made half-playfully, but Cooper promised his friend that a book should be written incorporating the scenery; as soon as he reached his home, he began its composition, and in three or four months had it finished. It is undoubtedly his best novel. He determined to make the risky experiment of reviving a character that had appeared in *Pioneers,* and he was justified by the climactic success of *The Last of the Mohicans.* By this he was naturally led to the composition of *The Prairie,* in which he killed and buried his hero. Cooper fully intended to leave him in his grave, but after thirteen years, the tremendous popularity of Hawkeye combined with the universal desire to know more of him, induced his maker to bring him back in *Pathfinder.* And finally he did what only a novelist can do to his hero, he not only resurrected him, but gave him his early youth, and in *Deerslayer* we see the future scout learning his craft among the lovely scenes of the lake at Cooperstown. All Americans who enjoy reading Cooper or their memories of reading him should visit the scenes of his stories; Cooperstown, Lake George, Glens Falls, Bloody Pond and the rest.

In reversing Time's flight with Leather-Stocking, Cooper developed his own powers of creation in due proportion to the strength and activity of the hero. He had only faintly shadowed forth the man in *Pioneers.* In contrast to the strong, resourceful, alert and adroit Hawkeye, it is a shock to meet the later Nat Bumppo; it is like meeting a friend after the lapse of years, and finding his youth and strength gone, and his fine spirit dulled. In *Pioneers* we have the picture of a rather ignorant and often plaintive man, who regrets the march of civilisation. The ideal side is missing. Every boy is homesick for Hawkeye.

In Leather-Stocking, Cooper added to the population of Immortals. He created a figure that will live as long as D'Artagnan, or Jean Valjean, or Pickwick, or Cyrano de Bergerac. He is an ideal, romantic, poetic character, so that all attacks on his "trueness to life" fall to the ground. Cooper afterwards knew exactly what he had accomplished. In the preface to the series, he said:

"The author has often been asked if he had any original in his mind for the character of Leather-Stocking. In a physical sense, different individuals known to the writer in early life certainly presented themselves as models, through his recollections; but in a moral sense this man of the forest is purely a creation. A leading character in a work of fiction has a fair right to the aid which can be obtained from a poetical view of the subject. It is in this view, rather than in one more strictly circumstantial, that Leather-Stocking has been drawn."

This statement completely disposes of the criticisms aimed at Leather-Stocking's failure as a human portrait. He is not a photograph—he is a hero of romance. No boy ever tires of him, nor any man who has anything of the boy left in his heart. He is more real in our memories than many historical figures.

All we can properly demand of a romantic hero is this: does he make a permanent impression on the imagination? That is the only test.

And if Cooper has been attacked for his Ideal

Scout, he has sufficiently been ridiculed for his Noble Red Man, especially by those who say the only good Indian is a dead Indian. And if wishes could kill, there would be few nations and not many individuals left on the earth. The death of nearly every person is desired by somebody. Cooper himself gave the final answer to the Indian's defamers:

"It has been objected to these books that they give a more favourable picture of the red-man than he deserves. The writer apprehends that much of this objection arises from the habits of those who have made it. . . . It is the privilege of all writers of fiction, more particularly when their works aspire to the elevation of romances, to present the *beau ideal* of their characters to the reader.

"This it is which constitutes poetry, and to suppose that the red-man is to be represented only in the squalid misery or in the degraded moral state that certainly more or less belongs to his condition, is, we apprehend, taking a very narrow view of an author's privileges. Such criticisms would have deprived the world of even Homer."

Even making due allowance for the romantic artist's privilege of idealisation, I do not doubt that the basal traits of the Indian were correctly given by Cooper. Mr. Walter McClintock, who lived with the Blackfeet Indians and was adopted into their tribe, has in his books unconsciously given striking testimony in support of Cooper's attitude. And our feelings about the good character of Indians will largely depend on our own attitude to them; it seems unintelligent to swindle or maltreat a person and then complain of his evil disposition. But had Cooper himself possessed no personal knowledge of Indians, he might have based his characterisations on Benjamin Franklin's incisive essay, *Remarks Concerning the Savages of North America*. Everyone ought to read this whether one is interested or not in Red-men. It is an important contribution to the literature of International Good-will, the only agency that can prevent war.

"Savages we call them, because their Manners differ from ours, which we think the Perfection of Civility; they think the same of theirs. . . . Having frequent Occasions to hold public Councils, they have acquired great Order and Decency in conducting them. . . . He that would speak, rises. The rest observe a profound Silence. When he has finish'd and sits down, they leave him 5 or 6 Minutes to recollect, that, if he has omitted anything he intended to say, or has anything to add, he may rise again and deliver it. To interrupt another, even in common Conversation, is reckon'd highly indecent. How different this from the conduct of a polite British House of Commons, where scarce a day passes without some Confusion, that makes the Speaker hoarse in calling *to Order;* and how different from the Mode of Conversation in many polite Companies of Europe, where, if you do not deliver your Sentence with great Rapidity, you are cut off in the middle of it by the Impatient Loquacity of those you converse with, and never suffer'd to finish it."

It is worth remembering, that not only does the *Leather-Stocking* series contain Cooper's best work because of the incidents in the woods, the characters of Chingachgook, Uncas, and their relations with the hero, but the only love-story in all his works that leaves a lasting impression, is the love of Cora and the young Indian chief. It would seem that only when Cooper is close to nature could he succeed in dealing with this natural passion. One would think it would be more difficult to portray love between a white girl and a savage than love between persons of similar race and breeding; and so it would be for most writers; Cooper is the exception. There is something elemental in the love of Uncas and Cora that gives this idyl a fitting place in the epic narrative. Love, like all instincts, is unaware of artificial barriers and social laws; in the universal language of youth, heart speaks to heart. The delicacy and restraint shown by Cooper in creating and in dealing with this situation is in marked contrast to the absurd modern cave-man and "red-blood" eruptions.

As Cooper was a pioneer in writing *The Pilot,* he holds the same honourable place in the *Leather-Stocking Tales.* He turned up new, unbroken ground, using purely American material. But although the ground was fresh in fancy, it was familiar to him in fact; he knew the woods as he knew the sea. And a good case might also be made for him in the statement that he was a pioneer in his management of nature as an integral part of his stories. It is not a background shoved in like a stage-set; he combines nature and man in a union so intimate that in his novels they cannot be divorced. Thomas Hardy simply did better what Cooper was perhaps the first to do well.

The chief faults of Cooper are faults of style, owing no doubt largely to haste in composition. He was not only no master of style, I doubt if he had any real conception of the meaning of the word. His English is chronically bad, and there are passages that seem to have been unconsciously designed as bad examples for young theme-writers. Slovenly, confused, involved, the second part of his sentences sometimes seems to have forgotten the first part. One of his recent editors has culled the following phrases, which must be almost the worst English that can be found in a masterpiece of fiction. They occur in *The Last of the Mohicans*.

"The eyes of the old man opened heavily, and he once more looked upwards at the multitude. As the piercing tones of the supplicant swelled on his ears, they moved slowly in the direction of her person, and finally settled there in a steady gaze."

This passage escaped from Cooper's pen, eluded him as he read the printed proofs, and escaped the revisions of the book. They are as hardy as a typographical error.

Yet there are times, when the inspiration was strong, that Cooper's style reaches a certain epic magnificence. The last chapter of *Mohicans* reaches a height of dignity and nobility.

His plots are not carefully constructed; they are more like a string of hap-hazard adventures. He must have "made it up" as he wrote. He sometimes contradicts himself, and is too fond of repeating the same device—everyone has noted the too frequent snapping of the dry twig. His adventures frequently pass the limits of credibility, his people sometimes act unnaturally, and talk even more so. His lack of humour was a limitation that is responsible for other faults. Stevenson was impatient of Scott's faults of composition, and yet regarded him with love and worship; Mark Twain's impatience with Cooper's defects made him blind to the abiding virtues. Both Stevenson and Mark Twain were meticulous artists; they slaved over their sentences, toiling in agony to produce the last finish and remove the faintest blemish; they felt perhaps a certain jealousy in seeing literary fame won without all this effort. Yet Mark Twain's slap-stick attack on Cooper is valuable only because of its humour. It belongs not to the page of book reviews, but to the comic supplement. It is undeniably amusing, but behind all the roaring mirth and saw-horseplay, Mark Twain was in deadly earnest. He seriously felt that Cooper had no place in literature, and that it was his business to drive him out. Inasmuch as many will read his specific objections without referring to the original paragraphs in

Cooper, I think it worth while to give two illustrations, to show how far from the facts Mark Twain's love of making a point would occasionally carry him.

From Mark Twain:

"For several years Cooper was daily in the society of artillery, and he ought to have noticed that when a cannon-ball strikes the ground it either buries itself or skips a hundred feet or so—and so on, till it finally gets tired and rolls.   Now in one place he loses some 'females'—as he always calls women—in the edge of a wood near a plain at night in a fog, on purpose to give Bumppo a chance to show off the delicate art of the forest before the reader. These mislaid people are hunting for a fort.   They hear a cannon-blast, and a cannon-ball presently comes rolling into the wood and stops at their feet. To the females this suggests nothing.   The case is very different with the admirable Bumppo.   I wish I may never know peace again if he doesn't strike out promptly and *follow the track* of that cannon-ball across the plain through the dense fog, and find the fort.   Isn't it a daisy?"

Mark Twain tells us that Cooper had a cannon-ball come rolling into the wood and stop at their feet, and that Bumppo promptly follows the track of that cannon-ball across the plain through the dense fog.

But this is the actual passage, in Chapter XIV of the *Mohicans*:

"He was yet speaking, when a crashing sound was

heard, and a cannon-ball entered the thicket, striking the body of a sapling and rebounding to the
earth, its force being much expended by previous re-
sistance.   The Indians followed instantly like busy
attendants on the terrible messenger, and Uncas
commenced speaking earnestly. . . . 'Tis soon
done, and a small hope it is; but it is better than
nothing.   This shot that you see,' added the scout,
kicking the harmless iron with his foot, 'has
ploughed the 'arth in its road from the fort, and we
shall hunt for the furrow it has made when all other
signs may fail.' "

Then, after hunting for some time,

"In this dilemma, Uncas lighted on the furrow of
the cannon-ball, where it had cut the ground in three
adjacent ant-hills.
    " 'Give me the range,' said Hawkeye, bending to
catch a glimpse of the direction, and then instantly
moving onward."

In this passage we see that the ball had done what
Mark Twain said it ought to do, that it was Uncas,
not Bumppo, who thought of finding the place where
it had last struck and bounded, and that the anthills
made the little furrow possible, thus giving the direction.   Unless one looked up the passage that
Mark alluded to, one would take his word that the
ball came rolling into the wood, stopped at the feet
of the party, and that Bumppo promptly followed
the track of that ball across the plain through the

dense fog.   And to take Mark's word here would
be doing an injustice to Cooper.

One more passage.   Mark Twain goes on to say,
in the same paragraph quoted above:

"If Cooper had any real knowledge of Nature's
ways of doing things, he had a most delicate art in
concealing the fact.   For instance: one of his acute
Indian experts, Chingachgook (pronounced Chicago,
I think), has lost the trail of a person he is tracking
through the forest.   Apparently that trail is hopelessly lost.   Neither you nor I could ever have
guessed out the way to find it.   It was very different
with Chicago.   Chicago was not stumped for long.

"He turned a running stream out of its course,
and there, in the slush in its old bed, were the person's moccasin-tracks.   The current did not wash
them away, as it would have done in all other like
cases—no, even the eternal laws of Nature have to
vacate when Cooper wants to put up a delicate job
of woodcraft on the reader."

Now this is what Cooper actually wrote, *Mohicans,* Chapter XXI:

"At length Uncas, whose activity had enabled
him to achieve his portion of the task the soonest,
raked the earth across the turbid little rill which ran
from the spring, and diverted its course into another
channel.   So soon as its narrow bed below the dam
was dry, he stooped over it with keen and curious
eyes.   A cry of exultation immediately announced
the success of the young warrior.   The whole party

crowded to the spot where Uncas pointed out the impression of a moccasin in the moist alluvion."

No one enjoys Mark Twain's humour more than I; but here again we are forced to believe that in dealing with Cooper he preferred to make a joke rather than to report accurately.   The matter would be of little importance were it not for the fact that Mark's attack on Cooper is fundamentally serious, and is based on examples which he has misquoted.   In the above passage, Chingachgook, or Chicago, becomes Uncas: instead of turning a running stream out of its course, he raked the earth across a turbid little rill which trickled from a spring.   Instead of the current washing it away, the "moccasin-tracks" were not there, and there was no current to wash them away; but after the trickle had been diverted, and the moist little bed dried, there was—to the sharp eye of Uncas—a faint print of a moccasin.

I think Cooper will survive Mark Twain's attack upon him.

Over against Mark Twain's derisive laughter, we may place the fine compliment of Stevenson, in the introductory verses to *Treasure Island.*

Cooper of the wood and wave.

Wilkie Collins, who understood how to tell a story, said "Cooper is the greatest artist in the domain of romantic fiction yet produced in America."   Balzac, after reading *The Pathfinder,* wrote to a friend, "It is beautiful, it is grand.   Its interest is tremendous.   He surely owed us this masterpiece after the last two or three rhapsodies he has been giving us.

You must read it. I know no one in the world, save Walter Scott, who has risen to that grandeur and serenity of colours. . . . Never did the art of writing tread closer upon the art of the pencil. This is the school of study for literary landscape-painters." Balzac also declared, "If Cooper had succeeded in the painting of character to the same extent that he did in the painting of the phenomena of nature, he would have uttered the last word of our art."

Cooper wrote too much. Had he written only one-fifth of the books he left behind him, he might stand higher. But his supreme merit is the *vital interest* of his best stories. He knew the art of suspense and the art of movement. The reader stops neither to admire nor to condemn, but turns the next page to see what will happen. We are led from crisis to crisis and have no time for reflection. We are not interested in his stylistic attitude, any more than we are in the grace of a man who is pointing a pistol at us.

Cooper's place in American literature is secure. He did what he could to injure himself, with his quarrels, his pamphlets, and his artificial novels of society. There is today all over the world a steady demand for the *Leather-Stocking Tales,* for *The Pilot, The Red Rover,* and *The Spy.* Cooper has survived many novelists in contrast to whom he seems uncouth, and he has survived his own crimes against the English language. *The Last of the Mohicans* is now a regular textbook in schools; and it will survive even that.

III

POLITICAL IDEALS

DANIEL WEBSTER AND ABRAHAM LINCOLN

DANIEL WEBSTER belongs not merely to American history and to American literature; he is a world-figure. He was a consummate statesman, and he is one of the foremost orators of all time, in the class with Demosthenes, Cicero, and Burke. His speeches show such a mastery of style as to give him a permanent place in literature.

Webster was born in New Hampshire in 1782. He had poor health in childhood, and forced physical inactivity gave him leisure for reading and private study. This love of books was one of the passions of his life and during his school days at Exeter and his undergraduate career at Dartmouth, he read constantly, making a speciality of history—the best early training for political service. He attained no high rank in the prescribed curriculum, but was prominent among his college mates as a speaker and debater. When he was eighteen years old, he delivered a fourth of July oration at Hanover.

He learned self-reliance by supporting himself through Dartmouth teaching, writing, and editing a newspaper. He was graduated in 1801, and in

1901, a week-long centenary celebration took place, which the Dartmouth authorities have incorporated in a handsome volume—invaluable to anyone interested in her greatest son.

It is my belief that Webster's entire political career was consistent from first to last. I do not share the common opinion that in the speech of the Seventh of March 1850, he turned aside from his previous course. He was always for the Constitution and the Union, and that much-abused speech was not only absolutely in harmony with his previous utterances—it was the wisest, finest, most patriotic, and most unselfish act of his life. Remember the two words—*Constitution* and *Union*—and you have the key to his conduct from boyhood till death.

About the time when he became of age, he delivered an oration in which he insisted on strictly adhering to the Constitution, no matter what section of the country felt injured. This stand was prophetic.

He studied law in Boston and was admitted to the bar in 1805. During the next eight years, he made many political speeches, in which he condemned the course taken by the national government—it was fiercely unpopular in New England—but, said he, "it is now the law of the land, and we certainly are bound to regard it." Those were the days when many in New England talked hotly of secession. Webster sympathised with their grievances, but was totally opposed to the idea of disunion.

He entered Congress from Massachusetts in 1813, at the age of thirty-one. Almost immediately he became one of the most powerful members of the House, being as conspicuous for brains as he was in appearance. No one failed to feel the impact of a new intellectual force. His statesmanship was shown by his mastery of that most difficult of all problems—public finance. This complicated question cannot be settled by rhetoric, oratory, or sentiment; but only by profound intelligence and prolonged study. He was always for sound money—and his services can hardly be overestimated.

It is the fashion just now to speak of Gladstone with contempt, as though he were nothing but a voice; it should be remembered, that he, like Webster, was a leading authority on public finance. This leadership comes only from cerebration.

Meanwhile Webster had risen to such eminence at the bar that he was universally regarded as one of the foremost lawyers in the United States. His position was still further strengthened by his notable argument in 1819 on the Dartmouth College Case, where he displayed complete familiarity with the facts and with legal technicalities, proved splendidly his loyalty to his Alma Mater, and by winning a decision won for American colleges what now amounts to many millions of dollars.

The full Report of the Case of Dartmouth College was published at Portsmouth in 1819, and fills a volume of over four hundred pages.

Webster was continually in public life from 1813 to his death in 1852. In 1827 he entered the Senate, in 1841 became Secretary of State, in 1845 was again in the Senate, and in 1850 once more Secretary of State.

The famous triumvirate is unique in history, and it is interesting to remember how closely contemporary were their lives.

Henry Clay,   born 1777, died 1852.
Daniel Webster, born 1782, died 1852.
John C. Calhoun, born 1782, died 1850.

Clay had extraordinary charm of manner, and enjoyed the largest personal following that any candidate for office has held, except James G. Blaine, Theodore Roosevelt, and William J. Bryan. But his presence was necessary to his speeches; it was he and not they, that triumphed. They cannot stand alone. Calhoun was a remorseless logician, whose speeches are chains of argument, one paragraph leading to another. His integrity and his intellect lent them force; but their rigidity and austerity make them hard reading. Webster alone of the three combined logic with grace, weight with suppleness. His speeches belong to literature because they are still not only readable, but thrilling.

Most orators are like actors. When the generation that heard them has vanished, they vanish with it. But Webster's last words were prophetic—"I still live."

Never was there a man who better looked the part. He was as impressive as a mountain. The Olympian dignity of his features, his superb car-

riage, his magnificent voice have become a tradition.
Dressed in the picturesque fashion of those days, the
blue and buff garments surmounted by the tall
beaver hat, he was more like a public institution
than a man. For once, Nature did everything to
make the individual complete, giving the massive
mind a fitting sublimity of corporeal expression.
One has to go to Shakespeare for an adequate description.

"What a piece of work! How noble in reason!
how infinite in faculty! in form and moving, how express and admirable! in action, how like an angel! in
apprehension, how like a god! the beauty of the
world! the paragon of animals!"

Thomas Carlyle met him at breakfast in London,
and wrote,

"I will warrant him one of the stiffest logic buf-
fers and parliamentary athletes anywhere to be met
with in our world at present—a grim, tall, broad-
bottomed, yellow-skinned man, with brows like pre-
cipitous cliffs, and huge, black, dull, wearied, yet un-
weariable-looking eyes, under them; amorphous pro-
jecting nose, and the angriest shut mouth I have
anywhere seen. A droop on the sides of the upper
lip is quite mastiff-like—magnificent to look upon;
it is so quiet withal. I guess I should like ill to be
that man's nigger. However, he is a right clever
man in his way, and has a husky sort of fun in him

too; drawls in a handfast didactic manner about 'our republican institutions,' etc., and so plays his part."

In his speech at the Dartmouth Centenary, the Hon. Samuel W. McCall said,

"There can be no doubt about the majesty of his personal presence. Business would be temporarily suspended when he walked down State Street, while people rushed to the doors and windows to see him pass. To the popular imagination he seemed to take up half the street. He stood nearly six feet, and seemed taller, and he had an enormous measurement around the chest. His head was one of the largest and noblest ever borne upon human shoulders. He had a dark complexion, a gunpowder complexion it was called, a broad and lofty brow and large black eyes, usually full of repose, but in moments of excitement blazing with terrible intensity. One of his severest critics, Theodore Parker, declared his belief that since Charlemagne there had not been such a grand figure in Christendom. . . . He possessed as noble a voice as ever broke upon the human ear—a voice of great compass, usually high and clear, but capable of sinking into deep tones that thrilled the listener. He made himself heard by nearly fifty thousand people at Bunker Hill."

Webster was a constructive statesman, who changed the course of history by talking. Even before the year 1830 he saw the cloud of civil war, then no bigger than a man's hand. I think he realised that nothing could prevent that cloud from becoming a destructive tempest, and hence he devoted his life to insuring the safety of the Ship of State when the tempest should break. A statesman is like a physician; the country is his patient; it is his duty to keep his patient alive as long as possible. His speeches built up an idea of Union so strong that it finally withstood the utmost fury of attack. I believe that if it had not been for Daniel Webster the people of what is now called the United States would be living under two flags.

Webster was against every foe of the Union, whether the foe called himself Southern Nullificator or Northern Abolitionist. Like all wise men, he believed in moderation, and had an abhorrence of extremists. He saw the folly of the agitators on both sides, and knew that the only way they could be silenced was by reason, by the appeal to fundamental common sense. When he said "Liberty and Union," he was not making a rhetorical flourish, nor uttering a platitude; he was stating a proposition that was constantly attacked by Northern and by Southern men; and he made it his business to prove that the slogan, "Liberty first and Union afterwards," was delusion and folly; there could be no true liberty in our country except liberty under constitutional law, under the flag of one united nation. Rather than Union, the Southerners preferred slavery and secession; rather than Union, the Northern extremists preferred abolition and secession; Webster made Union the paramount issue.

His Reply to Hayne in 1830 became the political bible of Northern farmers. They knew it by heart, for he had made the Constitution of the United States and the necessity of Union transparently clear to their understanding. Every speech that followed from his lips added something to the permanent structure, so that the Constitution became an organic whole, something worth living for, fighting for, and dying for. Thousands of Yankee farmers were prepared to debate the question whether the Constitution was the Supreme Law, or merely a compact between independent and sovereign states. When the political revolution of 1861 took place, public sentiment in the North was not only completely solidified, it was intelligent. The humblest workers were not like European peasants who knew not what they were fighting for, nor why; every man's intelligence was behind his enlistment.

The Reply to Hayne elevated the personal popularity of Webster to such a pitch that for twenty years he was canonised, and regarded with idolatry. Then came the speech of the Seventh of March 1850, and what a fall was there! His former followers engulfed him in a torrent of vituperation and calumny. The mildest epithets they had for him were "Time-server," "Apostate," "Traitor," and his friends walked no more with him. As so often happens in political life—which is one reason why decent and able men often refuse to enter politics—an enormous number of slanders against his private morality circulated with such speed and fury, that the air was full of the yapping of curs.

As a child, I was brought up to believe that Webster sacrificed the principles of a lifetime with the hope of personal advantage. How often I heard and how often I read the lamentation, "If he had only died before 1850!" I had, like all boys, declaimed the peroration of the Reply to Hayne, and had learned by heart many other fragments of Webster's speeches; but I did not dare read the 1850 speech, simply because I could not bear to see my idol fall. But one day, when I was seventeen years old, I determined that for my own historical information I must read that speech; this was the time when I began the excellent practice of finding out exactly what a man has said, rather than believing what his enemies said about him. I went to the original sources.

I shall never forget that day. I sat down, took up the speech, and fully expected to rise from the chair convinced that Webster was what Henry Cabot Lodge said he was, a morally inferior man, or at any rate, a man whose moral sense was not equal to his intellectual force. I read the speech from beginning to end, and at the conclusion, was filled with an enthusiasm for the great statesman compared to which my previous feeling was faint. The speech seemed to me then, and ever afterwards, as the noblest and most consistent utterance of his entire career. He was not a politician, engaged in palliative measures; he was a statesman, with his eyes on the future.

At that time, every history-book that I read, unsparingly condemned him; since then, it has been a pleasure to me to observe that the attitude of historians has changed to such an extent that to-day the most enlightened view of historical scholars is that Webster was both mentally and morally right. (To those who wish complete and detailed proof on this important point in American history and in Webster's life, I suggest that they read Professor Herbert D. Foster's admirable and completely documented article in the *American Historical Review* for January 1922, and the booklet, *Daniel Webster,* by Frank Bergen, a distinguished member of the Newark bar.)

Loyalty to the Constitution, so characteristic of Webster's earliest utterances as an undergraduate, as a Defender against Southern threats of secession, inspired this speech, when Northern Abolitionists insisted that the Constitution should be broken and defied.

The Seventh of March speech represents Webster at the zenith of his powers. It should be studied by every American boy and girl, as a text-book in preparation for intelligent citizenship. In addition to many burning questions, Webster answered for himself the question that every Senator and Representative must ask himself. Is my duty primarily to my constituents who elected me, or to the United States? This is an excellent subject for debate, for "much may be said on both sides."

In Anthony Trollope's little known but highly interesting novel, *The American Senator,* he makes

a slip which would betray the fact that even if we did
not know the author's name, we should know that
he was not an American. He invariably says
Senator *for* Minnesota, instead of Senator *from*
Minnesota. The little preposition displays the
vast difference between the method of representa-
tion in the British House of Commons, and our
National Legislature. One reason why the average there is higher than here, is because they have
Open Constituencies, which makes it possible to secure the best men, and ensures the country against
the loss of their services in the event of a local defeat. The moment any statesman in England is de-
feated in an election, a number of constituencies
come forward, and request that he do them the
honour of being their representative in the House.
With us, the Senator must reside in his state, and
the representative in his district. The advantages
of our system are, in my judgment, overweighed by
its drawbacks. I think it would be fine if any state
or district might choose the best man, regardless
of his residence; then we could have at Washington
a company of the ablest men in the country, met in
council for the best interests of the nation. So far
as local needs were concerned, a man of first-rate
ability could speedily discover them. I do not refer
to finding post-offices and other jobs for hungry
"political workers."

But above all, the attitude of a Senator toward
his office should be changed. Years ago, the ablest
prize-fighter of all time, John L. Sullivan, offered
himself as a candidate for Congress from a certain

district in Massachusetts. He said, "The business
of a Congressman is to get all he can for his constituents; and I can do that as well as anybody."
He expressed with his customary frankness and sincerity the silent creed of many of our public men.
The fact that many constituencies regard their
Senator or Representative as their political agent,
and that he agrees with them, is damaging
to both, and most damaging of all to the country
at large.

I believe that the essence of representative government lies in an intellectual attitude exactly the
contrary of this. We should elect the best men in
sight, and then leave them free to decide on what
measures are best for the United States, even if
at certain times a measure should be against the
wishes or supposed welfare of the men and women
who voted for him. A Senator should never be
bound by the demands of his state, if those demands
are against his conscience and best judgment.

This was the position taken by Daniel Webster
in the speech of the Seventh of March. Nothing
could be more absurd than the charge that he acted
for his personal advantage, for he was wise enough
to know that he was running counter to Massachusetts convictions. He regarded himself as a free
statesman, whose duty it was to exercise his own
private judgment, and follow it regardless of the
wishes of his constituents.

Without indulging in any cheap detraction of our
public men, it is probably true to say that the rarest
quality in public life is courage. It is a pity that it

should be so rare, for there are times when it even "pays" to be brave. Webster established a precedent; although he lost favour temporarily, that judgment against him has been reversed by the High Court of Time. There are occasions, however, when one does not have to wait for approval. In the recent struggle for Woman Suffrage, the New York Legislature instructed the two Senators from that State to vote in the affirmative. Senator Calder announced that with him the wishes of his constituents were mandatory; Senator Wadsworth defied them, on the ground that he could not vote against his own reason and judgment. His enemies cried, "The Lord hath delivered him into our hands!" But, although even his friends felt that his action had destroyed his political future, he was reelected by an enormous majority. And Senator Calder was beaten at the next election. In one of our states in the middle west, a representative voted against what seemed to be the sentiment in his district. A party of leading politicians in the chief town of that section sent him a joint letter, demanding that he appear before them, and explain his course. He replied that in his judgment he had been elected not as a rubber stamp, but as a free and independent political thinker; that he should invariably act and vote in accordance with his reason and conscience; that he did not conceive it to be his duty to neglect his work at Washington, in order to come home and defend himself against attack; but that he would always be glad to see any of his constituents in Washington who wished to call upon him, and ask him any questions. His doom was apparently certain; but he was reelected by an increased majority.

Senator Carter Glass of Virginia was threatened by a constituent with defeat if he did not vote for the bonus bill. His reply, as reported in the *New York Herald*, 25 February 1922, ought to be remembered.

"You must admit that you are distressingly wrong concerning the circumstances when you threateningly assert that I will violate campaign promises when I refuse, as I undoubtedly shall, to vote for the bonus bill. You are quite as completely mistaken in your supposition that I was sent to the Senate to act as the sounding board for any class of citizens which may assert, or imagine that it constitutes the majority of the people of Virginia. It is my conception that I was sent here to represent a sovereign State, to the best of my ability, according to my judgment and conscience, and not to trim sails to catch the shift of the winds of popular favor. I shall not vote for a bill which in my judgment would be ruinous to the country, embracing in its evil effects and numbering among its victims the ex-service men along with the rest."

It was the Seventh of March speech, which in a time of unbridled political passions, called upon the nation as a whole to stand by the Constitution, and the speaker himself set the example. This plea for moderation fended off the war for another ten years, when the North was strong enough to save the Southern states from themselves. Webster is practically called a moral coward by Mr. Lodge; but if his course here was wrong, what course should he have taken? Had he followed the clamour of his constituents, he would have broken his oath to support the Constitution.

He had previously defied his Massachusetts supporters, when he remained in the Cabinet of President Tyler. This happened in 1841, and those who condemn his attitude in 1850 on the ground that he was seeking personal advancement, ought to remember that nine years previously he had not hesitated to incur unpopularity and misrepresentation in order that he might perform valuable services to the whole nation. In the Dartmouth Centenary Book, the Hon. Stephen Moody Crosby gave his reminiscences of a certain evening in Boston.

"I was a boy thirteen or fourteen perhaps, when he returned from the Tyler Cabinet at Washington in political disgrace, to his friends in Massachusetts. The political story need not be repeated, but he came back to Boston and the cold shoulder was turned towards him with almost none to do him honor. A meeting was arranged in Faneuil Hall in order that he might make his statement as to why he had stayed in Tyler's Cabinet. My father who was a life-long admirer and lover of Daniel Webster took me there as a boy to serve out to me a part of that diet of Webster. I remember the crush. . . . I remember when Mr. Webster came upon the stage in his magnificent court dress, which he always wore on state occasions . . . a man who looked as Carlyle said of him, like a cathedral.   He came to the front when it was his turn to speak, and some one called for three cheers and they were not given.   One of them was given, the second failed in the attempt, nor was there any hand-clapping that would ordinarily be bestowed upon a man so prominent.   His eyes absolutely blazed.   They looked to me like two ship-lights at sea.   He began his speech in a calm conversational tone . . . but that as for him—and I wish I could recall his precise words as he drew himself up and said—'If there are any gentlemen here who expect to hear from my lips a word of explanation or apology for my remaining in the Cabinet of John Tyler, they are likely to go home as wise as they came,' and he roared it out through the hall in such a way that he dominated that great audience, and they gave him three cheers.   Before the close of the evening—he spoke about an hour and a half —they almost lifted the roof with their cheers and hand-clapping."

The speeches of Webster appealed to the mind and to the heart.   They are cogent in argument and almost irresistibly persuasive.   He possessed this intellectual and emotional combination to a higher degree than any other orator.   It is my conviction that the English language came from his lips with more appealing power than from the lips of any other person in the world's history.

The quality of his audience was never beyond his capacity. He could hypnotise an excited mob and he could make a Judge on the bench of the Supreme Court weep. He could sway a jury by a purely emotional plea; and he could clothe a legal abstraction so that it became a living thing. How often, I wonder, have the Judges of the Supreme Court found it impossible to control themselves, in the grasp of a sudden emotional appeal? They must often have been bored to the verge of tears; but to weep in public under the dint of pity? Webster is the only man that ever drew such a response, with the possible exception of Orpheus, who

Drew iron tears down Pluto's cheek.

His love of moderation, which made him hate and be hated by Northern and Southern extremists, is the ground-quality of his prose style. His self-restraint constantly suggests a vast reserve of strength; you feel that he can at any moment "turn it on." He is like a great singer, who gives the impression of always singing well within his powers. And as it is really painful to hear a singer continually doing his utmost, so it is distressing to hear an orator continuously screaming or continuously using superlatives. Webster never multiplied words without knowledge, and he made adjectives do their full work. It is surprising what results he obtained from the use of ordinary and commonplace words. E. P. Whipple, in his once-famous essay on Webster, noted the tremendous power that

Webster put into words like "interesting" and "respectable." He made himself and Dartmouth forever memorable by simply admitting that it was a small college. Was ever immortality gained by such simplicity? In his statement that it was small, and yet there were those who loved it, he put into a short sentence of short words the passionate loyalty of many generations. And as he could hypnotise an audience by common words, and accomplish that feat not by the tones of his voice but by the vast connotation he made the monosyllables carry, so he could make an object eternally sublime merely by pointing at it. He asked us to behold Massachusetts, and we did. The gesture illuminated all her history. In the Dartmouth Centenary Book, Judge David Cross, in speaking of the Bunker Hill oration in 1843, when he was in the audience says:

"Mr. Webster stood with his back to the monument, with fifty thousand or more people to the front and on the sides of him. I saw Daniel Webster as he stood upon the platform. . . . I remember him most clearly and distinctly as he stood there. I cannot tell the words. I shall not be able to give you an idea of it, perhaps, but as he stood before us he turned his face to the monument, his back to us, and said, apostrophizing the monument, 'That is the orator of the day.' I will not attempt to give his words, but the thrill that went through that audience, the thrill as I felt it at that hour has been with me from that hour to this. . . . As I have journeyed through the city of Boston since then, as I have looked at that stone monument, I do not know how it is, but every time I pass that monument it seems to speak to me. I cannot help it. The thrill goes through my veins as it did in 1843. That monument to me is alive."

Webster's style, with its simplicity and noble rhythm, is largely founded on the Bible, of which he had an intimate knowledge. In a letter from Cardinal Gibbons to the editor of the *Yale Review*, written 10 January 1920, speaking of a new book on the Bible which had just been reviewed by the Hon. Maurice Francis Egan, the Cardinal said:

"I am happy to see an interest taken in the Scriptures. Up to seventy-five years ago, the public men of our country seemed to have been saturated with the Bible. They were familiar with its contents and quoted freely text after text. Among many others, Mr. Webster seemed to have at his fingers' end the words of this inspired book. I remember to have counted in the pleading of Mr. Webster, counsel in the Girard Will Case, no less than 14 quotations from or allusions to Scripture. Apart from its inspirational character, the Bible still remains the one means of culture."

Webster was once asked what was the most desirable quality in a lawyer's equipment, and he replied "the power of clear statement." In dealing with the most complicated questions, public finance,

intricate details of boundary disputes, legal technicalities, and expositions of the Constitution, he made
his meaning and his interpretations clear to ordinary intelligence.   He often presented matters in
such a way that he seemed to have made a final and
unanswerable argument.   He was also a past master of the art of stating the position of an antagonist.

Underneath all his legal and public addresses was
the temperament of a poet.   It is the poetic quality
that makes his speeches live.   He gave ideality to
the point he wished to make.   He gave to the word
Union such vitality that when the Civil War finally
came, every Northern man felt that in fighting for
the Union he was fighting for some great Personality.

Daniel Webster died in 1852.   His work was
carried on by Abraham Lincoln.   Lincoln was not
an abolitionist, nor an extremist, and was hated by
both North and South as Webster had been.   He
followed the path made by Webster, and could not
be turned aside either by the threats of the South
or the remonstrances of the North.   His election
in 1860 is one of the miracles of history; but after
going through years of detraction that might have
broken the heart of a lesser man or weakened his
confidence in himself, we behold today a veritable
apotheosis.   Lincoln no more belongs to us than
Shakespeare belongs to England.   He is a world-
figure, and no list of the great men of all time would
omit his name.   He used to inspire certain in-

dividuals; now he is an inspiration to humanity.

Lincoln was the heir of Webster. He regarded the Union and the Constitution with his predecessor's eyes. Moderation, fundamental in both men, was then regarded as indecision and time-serving. Now we recognise it as the purest wisdom. What then seemed faltering we now know to have been firmness.

It was natural that the South hated him, for he stood colossally between them and their heart's desire. And though most enlightened Southerners today realise that he was their best friend, and that his death was incomparably a greater loss to them in defeat than to the North in victory, the old antagonism still occasionally flares out; an indication of the triumph of sentiment over reason, and of the vitality of Prejudice. In the *New York Times* for 23 June 1922, there is an allusion to a book written by a Southern woman, and its endorsement by a recent meeting of Confederate veterans. This book is an attack on Lincoln as a war-plotter; his Gettysburg speech is attacked as feeble in rhetoric; and his personal character is defamed. "Lincoln should not be held up as an example for Christian children."

All this is a little surprising just now, and yet, after all, quite natural. And it is interesting because it is human. Let it go at that. What I wish to show is the fact, that because Abraham Lincoln carried on the work of Daniel Webster, he was publicly attacked in the *North* and by Northern people

at just the moment when he most needed their support.

In 1863, at the darkest time of the war, Wendell
Phillips published a volume called *Letters and
Speeches,* containing reprints of the addresses that
this orator had made from 1860 to 1863. While
the war was going on, Wendell Phillips was holding
up President Lincoln to ridicule before Northern
audiences, and not content with saying such things
in the excitement of the platform, he collected them,
and published them in a substantial bound book,
bearing on its title page the date 1863. This work
seems to have been forgotten, but it is worth reading. I will quote from it.

"Not an Abolitionist, hardly an anti-slavery man,
Mr. Lincoln consents to represent an anti-slavery
idea. A pawn on the political chessboard, his value
is in his position; with fair effort, we may soon
change him for knight, bishop, or queen, and sweep
the board."

"The Union, then, is a failure. What harm can
come from disunion, and what good?"

"On the contrary, I think the present purpose of
the government, so far as it has now a purpose, is
to end the war and save slavery. I believe Mr.
Lincoln is conducting this war, at present, with the
purpose of saving slavery. This is his present line
of policy, so far as trustworthy indications of any
policy reach us."

"All civil wars are necessarily political wars,—they can hardly be anything else. Mr. Lincoln is intentionally waging a *political war*. He knows as well as we do at this moment, as well as every man this side of a lunatic hospital knows, that, if he wants to save lives and money, the way to end the war is to strike at slavery."

"It was a political move. When Mr. Lincoln, by an equivocal declaration, nullifies General Hunter, he does not do it because he doubts either the justice or the efficiency of Hunter's proclamation; he does it because he is afraid of Kentucky on the right hand, and the *Daily Advertiser* on the left. [Laughter.] He has not taken one step since he entered the Presidency that has been a purely military step, and he could not. A civil war can hardly be anything but a political war. That is, all civil wars are a struggle between opposite ideas, and armies are but the tools. If Mr. Lincoln believed in the North and in Liberty, he would let our army act on the principles of Liberty. He does not. He believes in the South as the most efficient and vital instrumentality at the present moment, therefore, defers to it."

"I do not say that McClellan is a traitor, but I say this, that if he had been a traitor from the crown of his head to the sole of his foot, he could not have served the South better than he has done since he was commander-in-chief [applause]; he could not have carried on the war in more exact deference to the politics of that side of the Union. And almost the same can be said of Mr. Lincoln,— that if he had been a traitor, he could not have worked better to strengthen one side, and hazard the success of the other. There is more danger to-day that Washington will be taken than Richmond."

"The President, judged by both proclamations that have followed the late confiscation act of Congress, has no mind whatever. He has not uttered a word which gives even a twilight glimpse of any anti-slavery purpose. He may be honest,—nobody cares whether the tortoise is honest or not; he has neither insight, nor prevision, nor decision. It is said in Washington streets that he long ago wrote a proclamation abolishing slavery in the State of Virginia, but McClellan bullied him out of it. It is said, too,—what is extremely probable,—that he has more than once made up his mind to remove McClellan, and Kentucky bullied him out of it. The man who has been beaten to that pulp in sixteen months, what hope can we have of him? None."

"With chronic Whig distrust and ignorance of the people, Lincoln halts and fears. Our friend Conway has fairly painted him. He is not a genius; he is not a man like Fremont, to stamp the lava mass of the nation with an idea; he is not a man like Hunter, to coin his experience into ideas. I will tell you what he is. He is a first-rate *second-rate man*. [Laughter.] He is one of the best speci-

mens of a second-rate man, and he is honestly waiting, like any other servant, for the people to come
and send him on any errand they wish.   In ordinary
times, when the seas are calm, you can sail without
a pilot,—almost anyone can avoid a sunken ledge
that the sun shows him on his right hand, and the
reef that juts out on the left; but it is when the
waves smite heaven, and the thunder-cloud makes
the waters ink, that you need a pilot; and today
the nation's bark scuds, under the tempest, lee-shore
and maelstrom on each side, needing no holiday
captain, but a pilot, to weather the storm."

"The policy which prevails at Washington is to
do nothing, and wait for events.   I asked the lawyers of Illinois, who had practised law with Mr.
Lincoln for twenty years, 'Is he a man of decision,
is he a man who can say no?'   They all said: 'If
you had gone to the Illinois bar, and selected the
man least capable of saying no, it would have been
Abraham Lincoln.   He has no stiffness in him.' "

"And so, when our rulers entered on the great
work of defending the nation in its utmost peril,
they dared not fling themselves on the bosom of
the million, and trust the country to the hearts of
those that loved it.   Your President sat at Washington, doubtful what he ought to do, how far he
might go.   Month after month, stumbling, faith-
less, uncertain, he ventured now a little step, and
now another, surprised that at every step the nation
were before him, ready to welcome any word he

chose to say, and to support any policy he chose to submit; so that matters of vexed dispute, matters of earnest doubt, the moment the bugle gave a certain sound, have passed into dead issues."

"But never will this rebellion be put down while West Point rules at Washington. [Applause.] It does rule. That second Commander-in-chief cuts off everything which outgoes his own routine."

"Let me make the Generals, and I don't care who makes the proclamations. Only let me put at the head of the advancing columns of the Union certain men that I could name, and the Cabinet at Washington may shut themselves up and go to sleep with Rip Van Winkle till 1872."

"Cease to lean on the government at Washington. It is a broken reed, if not worse. We are lost unless the people are able to ride this storm without captain or pilot. Yes, in spite of something worse at the helm. The President is an honest man; that is, he is Kentucky honest, and that is necessarily a very different thing from Massachusetts or New York honesty. A man cannot get above the atmosphere in which he is born."

"He means to do his duty, and within the limit of the capacity God has given him he has struggled on and has led the people struggling on, up to this weapon, partial emancipation, which they now hold glitteringly in their right hand. But we must remember the very prejudices, and moral callousness which made him in 1860 an available candidate, when angry and half-educated parties were struggling for victory, necessarily makes him a poor leader,—rather no leader at all,—in a crisis like this."

As a comment on these speeches, let us remember the letter from Abraham Lincoln to Horace Greeley.

"*August* 22, 1862

"I have just read yours of the 19th instant, addressed to myself through the *New York Tribune*.

"If there be in it any statements or assumptions of fact which I may know to be erroneous, I do not now and here controvert them.

"If there be in it any inferences which I may believe to be falsely drawn, I do not now and here argue against them.

"If there be perceptible in it an impatient and dictatorial tone, I waive it, in deference to an old friend whose heart I have always supposed to be right.

"As to the policy I 'seem to be pursuing,' as you say, I have not meant to leave anyone in doubt. I would save the Union. I would save it in the shortest way under the Constitution.

"The sooner the national authority can be restored the nearer the Union will be,—the Union as it was.

"If there be those who would not save the Union unless they could at the same time save slavery, I do not agree with them.

"If there be those who would not save the Union unless they could at the same time destroy slavery, I do not agree with them.

"My paramount object in this struggle is to save the Union, and not either to save or destroy slavery.

"If I could save the Union without freeing any slave, I would do it; if I could save it by freeing all the slaves, I would do it; and if I could save it by freeing some and leaving others alone, I would also do that.

"What I do about slavery and the colored race, I do because I believe it helps to save the Union; and what I forbear, I forbear because I do not believe it would help to save the Union.

"I shall do less whenever I shall believe that what I am doing hurts the cause; and I shall do more whenever I shall believe doing more will help the cause.

"I shall try to correct errors where shown to be errors, and I shall adopt new views as fast as they shall appear to be true views.

"I have here stated my purpose according to my views of official duty, and I intend no modification of my oft-expressed personal wish that all men everywhere could be free."

The letter to Greeley shows Lincoln's mind; the following letter shows his heart.

"Abraham Lincoln to Mrs. Bixby, Boston
            "November 21, 1864
"DEAR MADAM, I have been shown in the files of the War Department a statement of the Adjutant-General of Massachusetts that you are the mother of five sons who have died gloriously on the field of battle. I feel how weak and fruitless must be any words of mine which should attempt to beguile you from the grief of a loss so overwhelming. But I cannot refrain from tendering to you the consolation that may be found in the thanks of the Republic they died to save. I pray that your heavenly Father may assuage the anguish of your bereavement, and leave you only the cherished memory of the loved and lost and the solemn pride that must be yours to have laid so costly a sacrifice upon the altar of freedom.

            Yours very sincerely and respectfully,
                        ABRAHAM LINCOLN"

Hawthorne's portrait of Lincoln was made in 1862.

"By and by there was a little stir on the staircase and in the passageway, and in lounged a tall, loose-jointed figure, of an exaggerated Yankee port and demeanor, whom (as being about the homeliest man I ever saw, yet by no means repulsive or disagreeable) it was impossible not to recognize as Uncle Abe.

"Unquestionably, Western man though he be, and Kentuckian by birth, President Lincoln is the essential representative of all Yankees, and the veritable specimen, physically, of what the world seems determined to regard as our characteristic qualities. It is the strangest and yet the fittest ‘thing in the jumble of human vicissitudes, that he, out of so many millions, unlooked for, unselected by any intelligible process that could be based upon his genuine qualities, unknown to those who chose, and unsuspected of what endowments may adapt him for his tremendous responsibility, should have found the way open for him to fling his lank personality into the chair of state,—where, I presume, it was his first impulse to throw his legs on the council-table, and tell the Cabinet Ministers a story.   There is no describing his lengthy awkwardness, nor the uncouthness of his movement; and yet it seemed as if I had been in the habit of seeing him daily, and had shaken hands with him a thousand times in some village street; so true was he to the aspect of the pattern American, though with a certain extravagance which, possibly, I exaggerated still further by the delighted eagerness with which I took it in. If put to guess his calling and livelihood, I should have taken him for a country schoolmaster as soon as anything else.   He was dressed in a rusty black frockcoat and pantaloons, unbrushed, and worn so faithfully that the suit had adapted itself to the curves and angularities of his figure, and had grown to be an outer skin of the man.   He had shabby slippers on his feet.   His hair was black, still unmixed with gray, stiff, somewhat bushy, and had apparently been acquainted with neither brush nor comb that morning, after the disarrangement of the pillow; and as to a nightcap, Uncle Abe probably knows nothing of such effeminacies. His complexion is dark and sallow, betokening, I fear, an insalubrious atmosphere around the White House; he has thick black eyebrows and an impending brow; his nose is large, and the lines about his mouth are very strongly defined.

"The whole physiognomy is as coarse a one as you would meet anywhere in the length and breadth of the States, but, withal, it is redeemed, illuminated, softened, and brightened by a kindly though serious look out of his eyes, and an expression of homely sagacity, that seems weighted with rich results of village experience. A great deal of native sense; no bookish cultivation, no refinement; honest at heart, and thoroughly so, and yet, in some sort, sly,—at least, endowed with a sort of tact and wisdom that are akin to craft, and would impel him, I think, to take an antagonist in flank, rather than to make a bull-run at him right in front. But, on the whole, I like this sallow, queer, sagacious visage, with the homely human sympathies that warmed it; and, for my small share in the matter, would as lief have Uncle Abe for a ruler as any man whom it would have been practicable to put in his place."

Wendell Phillips had no conception of the real character of the man he befouled; and some may say that his blindness is excusable, because no one understood Lincoln. Unfortunately for Phillips, the beauty of Lincoln's character was appreciated by those who were in sympathy with him. On the morning after his nomination in 1860, the following tribute to the new candidate appeared in the *Chicago Press and Tribune:*

"One who has been led by providence through all the experiences of a lowly life, through labor and privation, through struggles and sacrifices, into self-reliance, into honest simplicity of life, into nobleness and purity of character, into a love of justice, truth and freedom that he might be fitted for the work."

Lincoln was not an educated man in the formal sense of the word; but for literary composition— of which he became a master—he was supremely well fitted. He had in the first place that love of truth and sincerity which is the foundation of all fine art; and he knew the Bible and Shakespeare so well that he could carry on conversations in quotation. Anyone who knows the Bible as Lincoln knew it has the best culture anywhere available.

The art of literary composition is the art of saying exactly what you want to say in a manner that will make it both clear and impressive to the minds of those who hear or read it. Lincoln's speeches and letters meet this test.

In his statesmanship and public life, Lincoln was a follower of Webster; in his character and dealings with individuals, he was a follower of the Light of the World.

IV

NATHANIEL HAWTHORNE AND PURITANISM

L IKE many men of genius, Hawthorne had no talent for the opportune. This indifference to "timeliness" he exhibited at the start, for out of all the 366 days of the year 1804, he entered the world on the Fourth of July. Never was there a man less of a jingo, less of a chauvinist; never was there one who viewed his native land with more cool detachment; never was there a quieter man, or one who hated more ardently the noise of guns and the noise of oratory; and it is characteristic of his shy humour that he should have been born among the reverberations of demagogues and the racket of firecrackers.

He was born in Salem and came of a long line of Puritan ancestors, one of whom was a Salem witch Judge. Although it will do no good, for the slander will go on circulating just the same, let it be repeated here that there never was any person in New England *burned* for alleged witchcraft. Some of Hawthorne's forbears were seafarers, his father being a ship-captain. The Puritan basis is so strong in Hawthorne that he was felicitously called by the critic R. H. Hutton the *Ghost of New England*.

He was graduated from Bowdoin in the class of
1825. That college has given more to literature
than any other institution of learning in America,
with the single exception of Harvard. One of his
classmates was Longfellow, and in the class of 1824
was Franklin Pierce, who afterward became President of the United States. It is rather remarkable
that in one small college there should be at the same
time among the undergraduates a future President,
the most popular of all American poets, and the
foremost literary artist of the Western Hemisphere.
Although the number of students was inconsider-
able, Hawthorne and Longfellow were but slightly
acquainted, moved in different sets, and were never
intimate. Hawthorne's closest friend was Frank
Pierce, to whom he was devoted all his life, and
for whom he actually wrote a Campaign Life—
as though Raphael should paint an advertising
sign.

Hawthorne was not a particularly brilliant or diligent student, but it is pleasant to remember that
his English professor had sufficient perception to
praise his original compositions. Nor was he dissipated, his head being strong and clear enough to
carry him safely through any company. On one
occasion, he was caught playing cards, and the two
letters he wrote home are so perfectly characteristic of his honesty, independence, and frankness,
that they are worth citation. He was wise enough
to anticipate the official warning by a private letter
to his mother, 30 May 1822:

"My dear Mother:—I hope you have safely arrived in Salem. I have nothing particular to inform you of, except that all the card-players in college have been found out, and my unfortunate self among the number. One has been dismissed from college, two suspended, and the rest, with myself, have been fined fifty cents each. I believe the President intends to write to the friends of all the delinquents. Should that be the case, you must show the letter to nobody. If I am again detected, I shall have the honor of being suspended; when the President asked what we played for, I thought it proper to inform him that it was fifty cents, although it happened to be a quart of wine; but if I had told him of that, he would probably have fined me for having a blow. There was no untruth in the case, as the wine cost fifty cents. I have not played at all this term."

(Then comes the sentence that no boy except Hawthorne would have written:)

"I have not drank any kind of spirits or wine this term, and shall not till the last week."

Any sensible mother would feel much safer after that definite statement, than if her son had written, "Mother, no drop of liquor shall ever again pass my lips."

His sister had evidently heard exaggerated reports of his misconduct, for on 5 August he wrote to her:

"To quiet your suspicions, I can assure you that I am neither 'dead, absconded, or anything worse!' I have involved myself in no 'foolish scrape,' as you say all my friends suppose; but ever since my misfortune I have been as steady as a sign-post, and as sober as a deacon, have been in no 'blows' this term, nor drank any kind of 'wine or strong drink.' So that your comparison of me to the 'prodigious son' will hold good in nothing, except that I shall return penniless, for I have had no money this six weeks. . . . The President's message is not so severe as I expected. I perceive that he thinks I have been led away by the wicked ones, in which, however, he is greatly mistaken. I was full as willing to play as the person he suspects of having enticed me, and would have been influenced by no one. I have a great mind to commence playing again, merely to show him that I scorn to be seduced by another into anything wrong."

It has always seemed strange to me that either students or their mothers should be willing to urge or to accept the plea of "misled by evil companions." That plea simply adds to the sin of misconduct the disgrace of cowardice. Hawthorne was so angry at the suggestion, that although he had no wish to play again, he came near doing so as an act of principle. This declaration of independence on his part was to characterise him all through life. He was intensely jealous of his intellectual freedom, and never permitted either his friends or mob sentiment to interfere with it, for he had rather lose the good opinion of others than his own soul.

Usually silent in company, he had that obstinate way of forming his own judgments that sometimes accompanies extreme shyness. He never felt the necessity of contradicting either with his voice or in letters-to-the-newspapers statements from which he loathingly dissented. He went his own way, quite unaffected by popular clamour, which had no more influence on his mind than if he had dwelt in Mars. He lived in troublous times, but there was nothing of the Reformer in him. Among all his Abolitionist friends in Massachusetts, he not only was not a Whig, he was content to remain a Democrat. He wrote to a friend:

"I regret that you think so doubtfully (or, rather, despairingly) of the prospects of the Union; for I should like well enough to hold on to the old thing. And yet I must confess that I sympathize to a large extent with the Northern feeling, and think it is about time for us to make a stand. If compelled to choose, I go for the North. At present we have no country—at least, none in the sense an Englishman has a country. I never conceived, in reality, what a true and warm love of country is till I witnessed it in the breasts of Englishmen. The States are too various and too extended to form really one country. New England is quite as large a lump of earth as my heart can really take in.

"Don't let Frank Pierce see the above, or he

would turn me out of office, late in the day as it is. However, I have no kindred with, nor leaning towards, the Abolitionists."

During the war, he visited Washington and the battlefields of Virginia, and wrote for the *Atlantic Monthly* an article called *Chiefly About War Matters,* which is amazingly aloof from partisanship. When we remember that John Brown had been canonised, that his soul was marching on, and that Emerson had declared that Brown had made the Gallows as venerable as the Cross, the following extract from Hawthorne's article in 1862 makes one pause.

"I shall not pretend to be an admirer of old John Brown, any farther than sympathy with Whittier's excellent ballad about him may go; nor did I expect ever to shrink so unutterably from any apothegm of a sage, whose happy lips have uttered a hundred golden sentences, as from that saying (perhaps falsely attributed to so honored a source), that the death of this blood-stained fanatic had 'made the Gallows as venerable as the Cross.' Nobody was ever more justly hanged. He won his martyrdom fairly, and took it firmly. He himself, I am persuaded (such was his natural integrity), would have acknowledged that Virginia had a right to take the life which he had staked and lost; although it would have been better for her, in the hour that is fast coming, if she could generously have forgotten the criminality of his attempt in its enormous folly. On the other hand, any common-sensible man, looking

at the matter unsentimentally, must have felt a certain intellectual satisfaction in seeing him hanged,
if it were only in requital of his preposterous mis-
calculation of possibilities."

I have given these political views at length, because they help to explain his novels. As he looked
on at his excited contemporaries in Massachusetts,
with the calm detachment of the observer, so he
looked on at life with the cool vision of the born
artist. Many readers, thinking of Dickens and
Thackeray, complain that Hawthorne has no sympathy with his characters; but if we remember his
political attitude we shall see that this is the same
man, regarding the children of his imagination with
no partisanship, but with the vision of an artist.
Whatever emotional excitement he felt was primarily artistic.

After graduating from Bowdoin, he spent twelve
lonely years at Salem, "the obscurest man of letters
in America." I know of nothing quite like this
in the career of a writer of genius, except the ten
years from 1832 to 1842, that Tennyson spent in
solitude, determined not to publish until he had
something that would satisfy himself. The American and the Englishman were silent at the same
period of time, and at the same period of their development—and never was self-repression more
richly rewarded. Though they were unknown to
the public, both men were working steadily at their
craft, writing, polishing, revising, destroying. Occasionally Hawthorne sent out a short story, for

which he received the munificent sum of three dollars, and no recognition.   He practically lived in
one room, living with the children of his imagination, living with his ideals and his dreams, and he
came to love that room as only an artist can love
a place where he has meditated and worked, and
where the air is peopled with the figures of his fancy.

On revisiting this place in 1840, he wrote:

"Here I sit in my old, accustomed chamber,
where I used to sit in days gone by. . . . Here I
have written many tales,—many that have been
burned to ashes, many that doubtless deserved the
same fate.   This claims to be called a haunted
chamber, for thousands upon thousands of visions
have appeared to me in it; and some few of them
have become visible to the world.   If ever I should
have a biographer, he ought to make great mention
of this chamber in my memoirs, because so much
of my lonely youth was wasted here, and here my
mind and character were formed; and here I have
been glad and hopeful, and here I have been de-
spondent.   And here I sat a long, long time, waiting
patiently for the world to know me, and sometimes
wondering why it did not know me sooner, or
whether it would ever know me at all,—at least
till I were in my grave.   And sometimes it seemed
as if I were already in the grave, with only life
enough to be chilled and benumbed.   But oftener
I was happy,—at least as happy as I then knew
how to be, or was aware of the possibility of being.
By and by, the world found me out in my lonely

chamber, and called me forth,—not, indeed, with a loud roar of acclamation, but rather with a still, small voice,—and forth I went, but found nothing in the world that I thought preferable to my old solitude till now . . . and now I begin to understand why I was imprisoned so many years in this lonely chamber, and why I could never break through the viewless bolts and bars; for if I had sooner made my escape into the world I should have grown hard and rough, and been covered with earthly dust, and my heart might have become callous by rude encounters with the multitude. . . . But living in solitude till the fulness of time was come, I still kept the dew of my youth and the freshness of my heart."

Perhaps no one ever understood himself better. The monastic seclusion of the little room preserved the shy sweetness of his nature, and gave to his style that bitterless austerity that is perhaps its chief charm. There is about all his work an air of serenity characteristic of so many timeless creations of art; this was largely caused by his prolonged solitude. Furthermore, his fecund imagination and economy in production are both shown in his statement that he had thousands and thousands of visions, of which only a few became visible to the world. So it ever was with him.

In 1841 he entered the Brook Farm experiment, where with the one exception of Charles A. Dana, he was most ludicrously out of his element. Yet he made of his experiences the *Blithedale Romance,*

the most permanent contribution of any kind that
Brook Farm gave to the world.   In a letter written
to Frank Farley (now first printed) he said in
1841 :

"Brook Farm, I suspect, is soon to see worse
times than it ever has yet—at least, so men of business appear to think.   Let it sink, say I—it has
long since ceased to have any sympathy from me,
though individually I wish well to all concerned.
                  Your friend,
                        NATH. HAWTHORNE"

In one respect he resembled most American authors; he married exactly the right sort of wife.
Nathaniel and Sophia Hawthorne had an ideal existence.   No one should ever give any extended account of the novelist's work without speaking of
her part in it, for without her inspiration and practical assistance it is probable that his best novels
could not have been written.   When he lost his
position in the Custom House, he came home, as
many a man has, to taste the very dregs of defeat—
to tell the woman waiting for him that he is a failure, out of work, with nothing for them to live on.
To his amazement, she greeted his dark tidings
with delight—"Now you can write your book."
And to his ironical query as to what they could
find to eat while he wrote, she opened a drawer,
and proudly exhibited a hoard of coins.   In response
to his bewildered question as to its origin, she told
him that for a long time out of the meagre sum

that he had given her every week for household expenses she had saved something, because she knew that her husband was a man of genius, knew too that the time would come when he would be without an occupation, and that this money would keep them both alive while he wrote his masterpiece. Was ever a wife's faith more nobly rewarded? Hawthorne sat down and wrote the greatest book ever written in the Western Hemisphere—*The Scarlet Letter*.

"It would be unpardonable," said Browning, speaking of the financial assistance he had received from his father, "if I had not done my best." Every page of *The Scarlet Letter* shows the inspiration not only of genius, but of a woman's love.

And now that we know what he thought of her, what did she think of him apart from her response to his genius? That response he could always depend on. When he read to her from manuscript the description of the death of Dimmesdale, she fainted. In the following tribute, remember that it is not a letter written during the honeymoon, but after eight years of married life. Is there any man in the world who can read this tribute of Sophia to Nathaniel without amazement and shame?

"He has perfect dominion over himself in every respect, so that to do the highest, wisest, loveliest thing is not the least effort to him, any more than it is to a baby to be innocent. It is his spontaneous act, and a baby is not more unconscious in its innocence. I never knew such loftiness, so simply borne.

I have never known him to stoop from it in the most trivial household matter, any more than in a larger or more public one. If the Hours make out to reach him in his high sphere, their wings are very strong. But I have never thought of him as in time, and so the Hours have nothing to do with him. Happy, happiest is the wife who can bear such and so sincere testimony to her husband after eight years' intimate union. Such a person can never lose the prestige which commands and fascinates. I cannot possibly conceive of my happiness, but, in a blissful kind of confusion, live on. If I can only be so great, so high, so noble, so sweet, as he in any phase of my being, I shall be glad."

Imagine a woman facing her husband every day at breakfast for eight years, and then having such an attitude toward him! The Ideal gained by close association; familiarity bred reverence. Truly, he had indeed kept the dew of his youth and the freshness of his heart.

Hawthorne's popularity outside of America suffers by comparison with that of Longfellow or Cooper, because his style cannot be translated. Still, the echoes of his masterpiece travelled swiftly across the ocean. *The Scarlet Letter* was published in 1850, and in 1851 appeared in Germany *Der scharlache Buchstabe,* and *Das Haus der sieben Giebel* came in the same year with the original, 1851. The demand was sufficient to embolden the publishers to produce *Zweimal erzählte Geschichten,* in 1852. In 1853 there was published at Paris *La Lettre Rouge,* while *La Maison aux Sept Pignons* came in 1865. In the twentieth century *The Scarlet Letter* was carefully translated into Russian *Krasnayia Bukvia.*

Hawthorne is our foremost creative literary artist; he stands alone, on the heights, with no one to challenge his preeminence. He is not relatively but absolutely great, and has an unassailable place in the front rank of the novelists of the world. His reputation was never noisy, but it has steadily widened, and increases with the increase of years. It is significant that he was the first American author to be included in the series *English Men of Letters.*

His originality is revealed in his Note Books, which should be read by all who are interested in him or in literature. They show an extraordinary wealth of material, so extraordinary, indeed, that if he had thought of nothing further, he could have gone on producing novels and stories for another century, using only what he had already outlined. What a quarry for modern magazine fillers! If any one doubts the genius of Hawthorne, let him glance through these Note Books.

He is original in his background, which he created for his own use. It is a background of sombre greys and browns, on which his brilliant figures stand out in sharp relief. There is a shadowy region which he has made entirely his own. It is not the ghoul-haunted region of Weir, for there is little in common between Poe and Hawthorne, however inevitable the comparison may be. The difference is that between the physical and the spiritual; Poe is uncanny, high-pitched, sensational; Hawthorne is subdued and subtle. To read him is to experience a change in the atmosphere rather than a change in the scenery. I see no reason at all for disparaging Poe, as many do, in order to exalt Hawthorne; they were both men of genius and a glory to American literature. But there is more humanity in Hawthorne.

His world of shadows is quite terrestrial; we do not really leave the earth. Over his creations hangs a thin veil of fantasy, poetry, romance, and we see his characters through this transparent, gossamer, silver-grey mist, analogous to the light covering the pictures of Andrea del Sarto. This atmosphere is never "worked-up," nor can it possibly be detached from the story, any more than the air can be lifted off the grass.

Hawthorne is what I should call an ideal realist. He is not a romance-writer, like Cooper; he is not primarily interested in happenings and adventures. Yet he is by no means a realist like Zola, nor for that matter like George Eliot; perhaps Turgenev more nearly resembles him than any other writer. It is realism seen through a poetic medium. "Fancy with fact is just one fact the more." "I fused my live soul and that inert stuff." He gives us a subtle psychological analysis of mental states.

It is seldom that a writer attains high excellence in both the novel and the short story. Irving, Poe,

Bret Harte and O. Henry left no long novel of
importance. Hawthorne was a master of both
forms of art.

His short stories are curiously unlike those that
adorn the magazines on railway bookstalls. They
are never "snappy." He was more interested in
the creation of character than in the manufacture
of incident. Now events move fast, while charac-
ter-development is a slow process. I can only imagine the impatience with which the army of popular—magazine-readers would struggle through a
typical tale by Hawthorne. Even in his own com-
paratively milder epoch, he realised that his stories
were too mild for the public. No one ever wrote
a better criticism of them than he himself.

"They have the pale tint of flowers that blossom
in too retired a shade,—the coolness of a meditative
habit, which diffuses itself through the feeling and
observation of every sketch. Instead of passion
there is sentiment; and, even in what purport to
be pictures of actual life, we have allegory, not
always so warmly dressed in its habiliments of flesh
and blood as to be taken into the reader's mind
without a shiver. Whether from lack of power,
or an uncontrollable reserve, the Author's touches
have often an effect of tameness; the merriest man
can hardly contrive to laugh at his broadest humor;
the tenderest woman, one would suppose, will hardly
shed tears at his deepest pathos. The book, if you
would see anything in it, requires to be read in the

clear, brown, twilight atmosphere in which it was written; if opened in the sunshine, it is apt to look exceedingly like a volume of blank pages."

This *uncontrollable reserve,* as he called it, marks the divergence between Hawthorne and many of our contemporary writers, who have an uncontrollable lack of it.   The word is apparently not in their dictionary.

Hawthorne's shyness is shown interestingly in such a scene as the dance-revel in *The Marble Faun,* which might instructively be compared with twentieth century dancing.   But the cold stiffness of that dance was not Hawthorne's idea of jollification; he knew exactly what he was about.   His austerity is shown in a more amusing way in his literary aversion to food.   I should like to write an essay on novelists from the culinary point of view.   Consider Dickens—his heartiness and gusto were so great that mountains of beef and seas of beer cover the pages of his books.   The reader of Hawthorne starves.

His prose style is the best ever produced by an American, and may be recommended for study to youthful aspirants with the same enthusiasm that marked Dr. Johnson's testimonial to Addison. There is in his language a musical cadence that never becomes a pronounced rhythm.   It is a harmony felt rather than heard, reminding one that "Heard songs are sweet, but those unheard are sweeter."

Perhaps no novelist has ever excelled Hawthorne

in analysis; yet he does not primarily depict phases of life or types of character. Men and women interested him as the embodiment of spiritual forces in conflict. When his genius is unencumbered by moral baggage, his analysis is most penetrating and revealing; in his less happy moods, he descends into rather obvious allegory. Allegory was ever leading him into temptation—it was a tendency that he had constantly to resist, for it was the easiest way. He had to struggle against his inherited love of moralising, as another man would fight an inherited love of drink.

His sense of humour and his restraint as an artist kept him out of the ranks of the reformers. The mistakes of zealots are gently satirised in *The Snow Image,* where the sentimentally sympathetic children bring the Image out of the cold in front of the cheerful fire, that It may share their comfort. Then to their dismay, It dies, killed by their benevolent intentions. Ibsen treated a similar theme less gently in *The Wild Duck.* One's own environment may not always be the most favourable for another's development. "God plants us where we grow," said Pompilia.

One of Hawthorne's favourite themes is the Elixir. The idea that youth could be renewed by some mysterious potion fascinated him, as this recrudescence has always been one of the dreams of humanity. In *Doctor Heidegger's Experiment* he makes the most of the dramatic contrast; and there is a certain poignancy in the fact that after his health broke down in 1860, and he saw Death advancing, Hawthorne should have begun and left unfinished *Septimius Felton,* a long romance based on this motive.

But his greatest theme is Sin—the lifelong struggle between instinct and conscience. *The Marble Faun* is mainly a study of the development of the soul through contact with sin. Hawthorne's Conception of Sin might be a subject for profound study. With all his artistic aloofness, the basis of his art as well as his own inner life was moral. He studies with a sad intensity the effect of sin on the human heart.

Sin is the theme of *The Birth-mark,* of *Wakefield,* of *The Ambitious Guest,* and negatively of *The Great Stone Face.* But the microcosm of all his work is to be found in *Ethan Brand.* So far as any tale could furnish it, we may find here the key to his own mind. This contains his driving idea, and exhibits in a nutshell his artistic process.

He got the hint by happening to see a lime-kiln in the night—how ordinary the sight, how extraordinary the result! But what is commonplace to the average man may be full of significance to the artist.

There are very few characters in *Ethan Brand,* and the interest is concentrated on one. By two or three incidents he skilfully suggests years of wandering.

In the Gospel according to St. Mark, III, 28, 29, we find these words of hope and terror:

"Verily I say unto you, All sins shall be forgiven unto the sons of men, and blasphemies wherewithsoever they shall blaspheme:

"But he that shall blaspheme against the Holy Ghost hath never forgiveness, but is in danger of eternal damnation."

This dark saying was for centuries a theme for theological discussion, enquiry, and exposition. There were many confident and hesitating interpretations, and many attempts to explain it away. Just as every Christian hoped that he was among the elect, so every Christian at times vaguely wondered if he had perhaps inadvertently committed the Unpardonable Sin. The two verses have thrown a tremendous shadow across human thought, and the theme is by no means obsolete.

When I was a child, I distinctly remember seeing the face of a man who was convinced that he had committed the Unpardonable Sin. I happened to be in an obscure corner of the room, where I could see without being seen. A young man entered, sat down on the sofa with my mother, and told her of his tragic predicament. I well remember how my mother tried to comfort him, assuring him with tender sympathy that the love of God was boundless and inexhaustible, that it was impossible that any believer and follower of Christ could escape from it, much less be condemned. She did not make the mistake of laughing at him, or treating his story lightly, for he had suffered and was suffering un-

speakable torture. She did not, however, with all
her gentleness, reinforced as it was by an almost
unparalleled knowledge of the Bible, succeed in
allaying his fear. He felt more certain of his fate
than a convicted murderer in the death chamber. I
have never been able to forget his face, as he went
out of the room in despair. Had he been actually
looking into the fires of hell, his expression could
not have been more hopeless and terror-stricken.
Of course the poor fellow eventually died in a mad-
house; but he was not mad then.

Ethan Brand has persistently sought for the Unpardonable Sin, and after searching throughout the
world, he finds that he need not have travelled at
all, for it is in his own heart. What then is the
Unpardonable Sin? It is "the development of the
intellect at the expense of the heart." Ethan
Brand had cultivated his mind until his emotions
were atrophied. The paralysis of feeling through
self-development is the theme of this tragedy.

The same idea is the basis of Tennyson's *Palace
of Art* and of Browning's *Paracelsus*. Why did
Hawthorne, Tennyson, and Browning lay such
stress on this particular by-way to hell? Because
they knew that they would never reach destruction
through the grosser vices; their danger lay in the
last infirmity of noble minds. Whatever may have
been the private thoughts of Tennyson, and Browning on this matter, it is all but certain that Hawthorne, with his temperament, realised his peril,
and wrote Ethan Brand and other stories to save
himself.

In his full length novels, as has been said, Hawthorne used only a small fraction of his material. Of the hundreds of plots that occurred to his mind, and which he set down in his Note Books, only a very few came to fruition. He left behind him only four completed novels, *The Scarlet Letter, The House of the Seven Gables, The Marble Faun,* and *Blithedale Romance.* Compare his slender production with that of H. G. Wells and Eden Phillpotts, who seem to have no difficulty in turning off three or four novels annually. And as Hawthorne gave us only four novels, so each novel contained as a rule only four chief characters. His method was not expansion, like Dickens, but concentration. Of the four books, only one, *The House of the Seven Gables,* contains more than four principals—that has five.

I do not share the opinion of those who place *The House of the Seven Gables* first, nor the opinion of Howells, who expressed his preference for the *Blithedale Romance.* I not only think *The Scarlet Letter* is his masterpiece, I think it is worth the other three books put together. The permanence of his fame hangs on this book and when we think of Hawthorne, we think of *The Scarlet Letter.*

The Introduction on the Custom House—which building was unfortunately burned in 1921—was written I suppose mainly to relieve his own mind. Here his ironical humour found a subject made to his hand. Little did the bench-warmers who decorated his office suspect that the shy man was shrewdly judging them, and storing them up for literary material.   As so often happens, both parties in these casual conversations regarded the other with secret contempt.   Hawthorne's advantage was in having an outlet.

Although the allegory is evident, it does not mar *The Scarlet Letter,* because the powerful individuality of the characters triumphs over it.   The story is greater than the moral, and the Individuals in it more impressive than any abstraction they might possibly be made to represent.   The allegory shows its head most distinctly in the chapter called *The Minister in a Maze,* but it can work no harm even there.   We are too deeply interested in the fate of the man, to turn aside into other paths of thought. And as *The Scarlet Letter* suffers when translated into another tongue, so it suffers when translated into another form.   The opera is one of the best ever written in America; Hawthorne's son-in-law, Mr. Lathrop, wrote the libretto, and Mr. Walter Damrosch the music, but their joint efforts fall short of the beauty of the original.   Richard Mansfield, one of the most intelligent and impressive actors in the history of the stage, mounted a dramatic version of the story.   He did his best, but while seeing and listening I could only think how much Hawthorne had lost.

Apart from the intense human interest of the narrative, *The Scarlet Letter* is remarkable as an expression of the sombre side of Puritan life. That was not the only side, for life went on its accustomed course even under Puritan domination. Young lovers kissed each other in the moonlight,

as they have always done; and there must have been
some frivolity, else why were such measures taken
to repress it? But the most striking, the most picturesque aspect of Puritan life, as we look back on
it from laxer times, was its gloomy austerity. I
suppose those who suffered the most were the children—for there was no place for them in the Puritan régime. Their mature masters would doubtless have heartily approved of the following peda-
gogic recommendations, given out by a German
moralist in the eighteenth century.

"Play must be forbidden in any and all of its
forms. The children shall be instructed in this matter in such a way as to show them the wastefulness
and folly of all play. They shall be led to see that
play will distract their hearts and minds from God
and will work nothing but harm to their spiritual
life."

The times have changed. Now the entire family
revolves around the nursery, where dwells the seat
of authority, and the desires of the child are the
law of the home. Probably the children are making the most of it, while the good weather lasts.

The sombre background of Puritanism brings out
the flame of *The Scarlet Letter*. The colours of the
book are a notable part of its scheme. Sunshine
and shadow in the great scene by the brook, where
for once the accursed letter leaves Hester's bosom,
youth and charm return to her face, only to retire
in defeat when Pearl refastens the symbol, when

all is again grey.   Pearl herself, the child of passion, flutters across the dark pages of the book, like
a brilliant, exotic bird across a sullen landscape.
For, in that cold New England community, she is
as exotic as a tropical visitor, coming as she does,
from a country not only unvisited, but unmention-
able.

Private sin was followed by public shame.   They
wore their rue with a difference, but they wore it.
In the Colony Records of New Plymouth, dated
June, 1671, we find (see Alice Morse Earle, *Curious Punishments of Bygone Days*), that the detected ones were forced

"to wear two Capitall Letters, A. D. cut in cloth
and sewed on their uppermost garment on the Arm
and Back; and if any time they shall be founde without the letters so worne while in this government
they shall be forthwith taken and publickly whipt."

Not only is this novel a study of Puritan life ex-
ternally—the spiritual foundation of the book is
Puritanism.   The consciousness of sin is the core
of the tragedy.   Momentary indulgence is followed
by prolonged mental torture.   The four characters
are linked indissolubly together by one caprice.   A
sin by many considered lightly, that has been the
source of vulgar jest since the dawn of history, and
made the object of religious worship by some an-
cient Pagan religions and by some modern novelists,
is here painted in the deepest grain; painted with
all its inevitable consequences.   As Goethe said,

Who never ate his bread in sorrow,
Who never spent the midnight hours
Weeping and watching for the morrow,
He knows ye not, ye gloomy powers.

To earth, this weary earth, ye bring us:
To guilt ye let us heedless go,
Then leave repentance fierce to wring us:
A moment's guilt, an age of woe!

There are many who rebel fiercely against what they regard as the unfairness of the punishment, for there are many who are forever trying to play the game of life without obeying the rules.

Had the Puritan Jonathan Edwards written the book, instead of the cool artist Hawthorne, he could not have depicted sin in more powerful language. Thus I could wish that Hawthorne had not added the final chapter, but had let the book close with the dying confession of the minister, and its echo from the crowd.

George Woodberry says, "It is a relentless tale; the characters are singularly free from self-pity, and accept their fate as righteous; they never forgave themselves, they show no sign of having forgiven one another; even God's forgiveness is left under a shadow of futurity. . . . A book from which light and love are absent may hold us by its truth to what is dark in life; but, in the highest sense, it is a false book."

I dislike to differ from so profound and thoughtful a critic, and from one who adds to his critical perception so sure a sense of moral values. But here he misses the point. To answer his main contention, all we have to do is to regard Chillingworth, remembering that it was often Hawthorne's way to show an idea negatively. Chillingworth is transformed from a calm, benign scholar, with the impersonal expression of an investigator, into a veritable fiend; hell has complete dominion over him, and his eyes reflect the glare of the pit. This degradation is brought about purely by the subtle poison of revenge; simply because he cannot forgive, and thus be free. His face changes by the slow cancer of hate into something inhuman. Observe that he never wants the minister to confess; for the moment Dimmesdale confesses, he ceases to be his slave.

Light and love are not absent from the book; over the scaffold there is a celestial glory. And the objection of Mr. Woodberry, that "the characters are singularly free from self-pity," is not this one of Hawthorne's greatest triumphs? Think of the vast number of people today, in and out of novels, who insist on their "right to happiness," no matter by what degradation it is attained, nor by what pain caused to others. Arthur and Hester were made of sterner stuff, as became the age in which they lived, as became their profound sense of responsibility, as became their respect for each other's soul. They were free from the insidious weakness of self-pity. They took life seriously. They knew they had sinned, and sought no excuse—

how entirely different they were from those who regard their misconduct with complacency! "Such is
the way of the adulterous woman; she eateth, and
wipeth her mouth, and saith, I have done no wicked-
ness." The ways of such women were beyond the
understanding of Agur, but he would have understood Hester.

Another leading idea in the book is the contrast
between the loss of public respect and the loss of
private respect, self-respect. Hester suffers the
worst possible punishment that may befall a woman
—public ostracism. There are those who say they
do not care what anybody thinks of them; granting
that they are speaking truly, a difficult admission,
how if such a one were shunned on the streets as if
he had some disgusting and contagious disease?
How if every public appearance meant the derisive
hooting by small boys, the studious crossing to
the other side by former acquaintances, enforced
isolation worse than a prison cell? This is what
Hester, a young and lovely woman, has to endure.
But the worst has happened; she at all events has
nothing worse to fear; and her punishment is not
greater than she can bear, for in the scarlet letter
she carries both her sin and its expiation. She suffers more on the street than in the solitude of her
own room. There she has peace of mind.

Compared with the minister, she is enviable.
He is the public idol. What gall, what wormwood,
it must be to him to hear his praises sung to his face,
to be told by adoring parishioners of the good his
sermons have wrought, to be saluted on the street

with all the marks of reverence—and to know in his
own heart what he really is, to have the scarlet letter
burning in his breast! How intolerable his solitude must be as compared with that of Hester!

I do not think we need to envy anyone who has
paid for success with the loss of character. What
must such people think when they look in the mirror,
provided, of course, that any rag of decency remains? In a certain sense, we are all hypocrites;
no one lives up to his ideal. But I take it that most
of us on the whole are sincere; that we do not deliberately preach one doctrine and practice another.
Perhaps many a man has tried to comfort himself
with the vain hope that his words may do good,
even though his life be evil; as Schopenhauer, who
taught asceticism and practiced the contrary, urged
that readers follow his precepts and not his example.
Unfortunately for such self-deceived worthies, the
world invariably selects for the first test of a man's
doctrine, the behaviour of the man who preaches it.
And the world is right; for if it fails in the life of
its sponsor, where may one hope that it will be fruitful? No, sincerity and truth are cardinal virtues.

Not only is the book a revelation of spiritual
forces, the powers in the air, but even the bodies
of the chief actors express their souls. This has
already been pointed out in the case of Chillingworth; consider the varied thoughts of Hester in her
varied meetings with Arthur, and how her face
changes with them; consider the minister, with his
hand on his heart, his body wearing thin from the
inner fire till it becomes almost transparent; consider

the whimsical fancies of Pearl, and how they are re-
flected in her eyes. Such presentations remind us
of the words of Donne, speaking of the young girl:

> *Her pure and eloquent blood*
> *Spoke in her cheeks, and so distinctly wrought.*
> *That one might almost say, her body thought.*

It is instructive by contrast to compare Flaubert's
Madame Bovary with Hawthorne's *Scarlet Letter*.
They were both equally deliberate artists, and their
prose styles are equally excellent. In *Madame
Bovary*, surely a great work of art, we have a miserable picture of sordid degeneration ending in blank
despair. Life has no solution. In *The Scarlet
Letter*, we have sin and its consequences, illumined
at last by the light of heaven. Henry James said
that *Madame Bovary* would make a good Sunday-
school book, and indeed it is far more sincere and
therefore moral than many of the novels written
professionally in that manner. But Flaubert has
nothing but scorn for his characters, whereas Hawthorne treats all of his people with dignity and respect. He did not show the sympathy with his
characters that we find in Dickens and Thackeray,
but he was deeply moved by their fate, quite apart
from his skill in managing it.   I cannot help thinking
that in his recommendation, Henry James knew
more about French fiction than he did about Sunday-
schools.
There is another profound difference between
these two masterpieces.   Flaubert was interested in

the sin itself, and is not sparing of details. Hawthorne is interested only in the mental consequences.
Hence he purposely began his story after the crime,
in order to concentrate wholly on the spiritual and
mental results. It is all falling action. Hawthorne
perhaps meant to show that the effects could not be
separated from the cause.

The evolution of the story is flawless. The plot
unfolds as naturally and with as little apparent effort as the petals of a flower. In this respect, Hawthorne is superior to Balzac; for in the works of the
French giant we feel the expense of energy. Here
we have a natural beginning, a natural development,
with an inexpressibly affecting conclusion. *The
Scarlet Letter* illustrates Thomas Hardy's definition
of a novel, that it should be a living organism.

Observe how the author introduces a new movement into the complications; there is no side remark
to the reader; there is no sensational clap-trap; no
attempt to startle or confuse. For example, the
fact that Chillingworth has engaged passage on the
same ship is absolutely vital, destructive as it is to
the plans of the lovers; yet it slips into place so
naturally that one feels that the story has not been
constructed at all, but is silently growing to fruition.
The revelation is a noble climax:

"My little Pearl," said he feebly,—and there
was a sweet and gentle smile over his face, as of a
spirit sinking into deep repose; nay, now that the
burden was removed, it seemed almost as if he would
be sportive with the child,—"dear little Pearl, wilt

thou kiss me now? Thou wouldst not, yonder in the forest! But now thou wilt?"

Pearl kissed his lips. A spell was broken. The great scene of grief, in which the wild infant bore a part, had developed all her sympathies; and as her tears fell upon her father's cheek, they were the pledge that she would grow up amid human joy and sorrow, nor forever do battle with the world, but be a woman in it. Towards her mother, too, Pearl's errand as a messenger of anguish was all fulfilled.

"Hester," said the clergyman, "farewell!"

"Shall we not meet again?" whispered she, bending her face down close to his. "Shall we not spend our immortal life together? Surely, surely, we have ransomed one another with all this woe! Thou lookest far into eternity, with those bright dying eyes! Then tell me what thou seest?"

"Hush, Hester, hush!" said he with tremulous solemnity. "The law we broke!—the sin here so awfully revealed!—let these alone be in thy thoughts! I fear! I fear! It may be that, when we forgot our God,—when we violated our reverence each for the other's soul,—it was thenceforth vain to hope that we could meet hereafter, in an everlasting and pure reunion. God knows; and He is merciful! He hath proved his mercy, most of all, in my afflictions. By giving me this burning torture to bear upon my breast! By sending yonder dark and terrible old man, to keep the torture always at red-heat! By bringing me hither, to die this death of triumphant ignominy before the people! Had either of these agonies been wanting, I had been lost forever! Praised be his name! His will be done! Farewell!"

That final word came forth with the minister's expiring breath. The multitude, silent till then, broke out in a strange, deep voice of awe and wonder, which could not as yet find utterance, save in this murmur that rolled so heavily after the departed spirit.

V

THE AMERICAN PHILOSOPHER
RALPH WALDO EMERSON

SOME years ago, I asked a Japanese student who had just entered Yale, what motive had impelled him to leave his native land and come hither to study. He replied that in Tokyo he had come across a book by Ralph Waldo Emerson which had been translated into Japanese, and the contents had made such an impression upon his mind that he had immediately vowed to see for himself the country that produced such a man. Here is an instance out of many thousands where the living word of our great Practical Mystic has awakened and transformed an individual of another time and clime. For our foremost American individualist always spoke to individuals, never to men in the mass; thus every one who reads him receptively feels that the stimulating word is addressed to him alone.

In the year 1803 Emerson was born on Summer Street, Boston, near what is now the South Terminal Station. Can you think of three men of genius more unlike than Benjamin Franklin, Edgar Allan Poe, and Ralph Waldo Emerson? All three were born in Boston, though only the last is really identified with it. Emerson always loved Boston, and in one of his worst poems, he exclaims

This darling town of ours.

Emerson is the only one of the three who ought to have been born in Boston. Franklin never felt at home there and Poe never felt at home anywhere. But the atmosphere of the Athens of America suited Emerson. Smile as much as you like, but Boston is *different.* The street-cars show it in three striking peculiarities: the strap-hangers read bound books, not newspapers and grotesque magazines; the signs proclaim that this is a Prepayment Car, which would not be understood in many other towns; the conductors say *Madam,* instead of *Lady.* I was once having my boots blacked, or my shoes shined— according as you prefer the British or American alliteration—and the tiny Boston polisher, who had thus far served a life sentence of not less than five nor more than ten years suddenly asked me what I thought of the Philippines; "for my part," said he, "they seem more of a liability than an asset."

On his father's side, Emerson came of eight successive generations of ministers, giving him a sufficient supply of ethics and religion; on his mother's side, his grandfather was a whiskey distiller, who had "no ancestry" but left forty-six grandchildren. The high percentage of practical wisdom in Emerson may possibly be partly owing to this eminently practical man.

Emerson was a rather abnormal boy who lived at home, had no intimate playmates, no Indian warwhoops, no picnics, and no adventures. Neither in school nor college did he take part in any sports or athletic contests, nor did he ever pretend to care for such things. Emerson reading the sporting page of a newspaper is unthinkable. He studied and meditated incessantly.

He was graduated from Harvard in the class of 1821. In the long roll of illustrious sons of Harvard, Emerson is perhaps the most illustrious and certainly the most influential. But his undergraduate days were not happy. He was "President's Freshman"—a hired messenger. This provided him with a free room in Wadsworth House, thus saving the expense of lodging. He did private tutoring, taught school in vacation and waited on table in term-time. The last three years he roomed in Hollis, but lived as much by himself as was possible in a college dormitory. He made little impression on either students or faculty, was never prominent and not thought to be a young man of any particular promise. His health was not rugged, and he never looked back to his undergraduate days with much pleasure, or rated his "education" very highly, the almost invariable attitude of a super-individualist.

Years later, when Emerson was an Overseer of Harvard College, he voted in favor of compulsory chapel. His latest biographer, the learned and ingenious Professor Firkins, rebukes Emerson for this vote, saying that while it may not be a blot on his record it is certainly a blur. I cannot subscribe to this opinion. Emerson was certainly an individualist, and a believer in personal freedom; but he also believed that Religion was the most important part of any one's education and the chief element in life. Thus his vote seems to me consistent with his general mental attitude, though I should not care if it were not.   Consistency was never a jewel with Emerson.

We are now fortunate enough to possess the numerous volumes of his Journal, published not long ago, which illumine his inner life, and are full of good anecdotes.   As Dr. Johnson wrote disparagingly of New Jersey, so Emerson gave a delightful opinion of Connecticut.   In 1862 he met Mrs. John C. Frémont at Washington.

"She showed me two letters of her son who had once been designed for our Concord School, but when she came to find how much his reading, spelling, and writing had been neglected in his camp education . . . she was afraid to send him among cultivated boys, and had sent him into Connecticut."

Emerson could upon occasion hand down an opinion from the seat of the scornful, as when he followed the advice of political economists:

"I took such pains not to keep my money in the house, but put it out of the reach of burglars by buying stock, and had no guess that I was putting it into the hands of those very burglars now grown wiser and standing dressed as Railway Directors."

When he was eighteen, he wrote,

"Why has my motley diary no jokes? Because it is a soliloquy and every man is grave alone."

Perhaps true of some men, but not of all. I feel sure that the author of the *Anatomy of Melancholy* was often enormously amused by his solitary reflections on human nature.

When he was eighteen, he indulged himself in the following lament:

"In twelve days I shall be nineteen years old: which I count a miserable thing. Has any other educated person lived so many years and lost so many days?"

It is forever characteristic of humanity that the more serious and ambitious a person is, the more he is given to self-reproach. Consider Milton's Sonnet on his twenty-third birthday. It is the energetic who condemn themselves for laziness, the saints who suffer remorse for their sins. The real loafer and the genuine criminal are self-complacent, and leave the art of worrying to their betters.

As everyone knows, Emerson was a Unitarian minister, and he might have continued in that profession if it had not been for three things: he disliked all confessions of faith, he disliked preaching in the pulpit, and he particularly disliked pastoral work. It was once necessary for him to make a call on an old parishioner who was engaged in the serious business of dying. The young pastor sat by the bedside, and could think of nothing to say.   After stammering out a few non-committal generalities, the old fellow cried out peevishly, "Young man, if you don't know your business, you had better go home."   Emerson, who had come to give advice, not only received it, but immediately acted upon it, like the sensible person he was; and soon he left the ministry altogether, being certain that in an occupation where he was chronically uncomfortable, he could not be successful.   He was too much of an individualist to feel at home in any organisation— he could inspire, but he could not cooperate.

From the quiet village at Concord he fired the shot heard round the world.   From that retreat, he sallied forth as a Lyceum Lecturer, perhaps the greatest America has ever known.   He lectured in England and New England, mid-western villages, and along the coast of California.   Lowell's essay on *Emerson the Lecturer* brings his personal presence visibly before us.

In his later years his reason became clouded; the most thrilling account of him in this tragic condition is to be found in *The Americanization of Edward Bok.*

He died at Concord in 1882.   A boulder properly marks the grave, and the inscription thereupon is characteristically obscure to those unfamiliar with his philosophy.

The passive master lent his hand
To the vast soul that o'er him planned.

If any who read this account of him are puz-
zled by the two lines, I refer them to Emerson's
poem, *The Problem*.

The Concord School is perhaps the only School
of writers America has produced, though the state
of Indiana has furnished a group. Concord has
done more for literature than New York, as Wei-
mar did more than Berlin. Emerson was the Head:
his chief disciple was Thoreau, whose fame brightens
with the passage of time; Margaret Fuller and the
Alcotts (A. Bronson Alcott's chief contribution to
the world was Louisa) of course belong there; Hawthorne lived in Concord, and the whole New England galaxy were profoundly influenced by the
emanations from the village.

The school of thought, beginning in Unitarianism,
went into Transcendentalism, and thence into practical movements like Abolitionism and social re-
form. Concord became the Mecca of the eccen-
trics. Radical ideas in politics, sociology, philosophy, and religion filled the air, and every male and
female Oddity in America who could find the means
of transportation journeyed to Concord. Emerson
was never disturbed by hostile criticism; his suffer-
ings came from his disciples. In this Paradise of
Cranks he moved with a serenity all his own. Fundamental common-sense and a certain homely,
shrewd humour saved him from the excesses into
which his teaching led those who were less balanced.
When Thoreau was jailed for his political principles, Emerson went to see him, and was shocked at

the apparition behind the bars.   To his sorrowful question, "Henry, why are you here?" came the defiant rejoinder, "Why are you not here?"

Emerson was always practical, always punctiliously courteous.   His bold ideas did not spoil his good manners.   When the dinner bell rang, he instantly laid down his pen, even if he were in the midst of the sentence; it was not right to keep anyone waiting.   A reformer called upon him with his hat on. Emerson asked him if he would not remove it, and the visitor said he uncovered only before God.   Then Emerson pleasantly suggested that they both go out and talk in the garden.   In the following language, Emerson described a certain convention.

"Madmen, mad women, men with beards, Dunkers, Muggletonians, Come-Outers, Groaners, Agrarians, Seventh-day Baptists, Quakers, Abolitionists, Calvinists, Unitarians, and Philosophers."

The man who could describe a convention in that spirit is plainly not committed to it.

Emerson was not a philosopher like Kant or Schopenhauer or Berkeley or Josiah Royce.   He was not a System-Maker, and there is no real or pretended scientific basis for his ideas.   He was a philosopher in the etymological sense—a Lover of Wisdom.   He was a fine exponent of plain living and high thinking, less pretentious but more consistent than Tolstoi.   He was serene in both life and mind.

He *announced* truths, and was so sure of them it was indifferent to him whether they were accepted or not.   He had little of the spirit of propaganda in him, knowing that the truth would ultimately prevail.   He refused to argue and declined to explain. His only basis was intuition.   As a realistic novelist reports what he sees in the natural world, so Emerson reported what he saw with the eye of the spirit.   In response to a request for details, he wrote,

"I could not give account of myself if challenged. I could not possibly give you one of the arguments you cruelly hint at, on which any doctrine of mine stands: for I do not know what arguments mean in reference to any expression of a thought.   I delight in telling what I think: but if you ask me how I dare say so, or why it is so, I am the most helpless of mortal men."

In his own mental poise, he seems to me to have belied one of his most profound utterances—"God offers to every mind its choice between truth and repose.   Take which you please—you can never have both."   In some fashion as inexplicable as his intuitions, he managed without compromising to take both.

So far as I can grasp it, he believed that the Divine Personality included everything.   Nature and man are both divine.   Man is the voice and Nature the hand-writing of God.   Every man is potentially God.   His divergence from Christianity

appears in his conviction that Jesus Christ was not
divine and became human; He was human and became divine.

The result of all this is wholesale and uncompromising optimism. He smiled at Carlyle's de-
nunciations, and when the stark Scot took him
through the nocturnal horrors of London, like Vir-
gil escorting Dante through hell (what a pair to
go slumming!) Emerson remarked that all this
was working out in accordance with the Divine plan.
Like his own Humble Bee, he extracted honey from
every book he read and everything he saw. He
left the chaff and took the wheat. He simply could
not "take" evil, no matter how often he might be
exposed to it.

> *Here the blot is blanched*
> *By God's gift of a purity of soul*
> *That will not take pollution, ermine-like*
> *Armed from dishonour by its own soft snow.*
> *Such was this gift of God who showed for once*
> *How He would have the world go white.*

When Fanny Ellsler delighted and shocked Bos-
ton with her brilliant ballet-dancing, Emerson and
Margaret Fuller went together to see her perform.
In the midst of the spectacle, she whispered,
"Waldo, this is poetry." And the reply: "Hush,
Margaret, it is religion!"

As Woodberry has pointed out—the same is true
of Wordsworth—there was in Emerson a combination of the universal with the intensely local. His

mind was free of the limits of time and space; yet he was strongly identified with Boston and Concord, and content to be.

But he was by no means only a dreamer. On the local side, he had common sense and Yankee shrewdness. He was an observer as well as a mystic. *Representative Men* shows his clear judgment; *English Traits* his shrewdness.

It is curious that the two friends, Emerson and Carlyle, should each have produced early in life a book that contained in little so much of their philosophy that all their subsequent publications are mainly expansive and annotative. These two books are Emerson's *Nature* published in 1836, and Carlyle's *Sartor Resartus,* published in 1834. Neither ever departed from the principles there laid down; they simply developed them.

It took eleven years to sell five hundred copies of *Nature,* which shows that the influence of a book may be in inverse proportion to its commercial success. Carlyle instantly recognised the significance of his friend's work. He wrote,

"Your little azure-colored *Nature* gave me true satisfaction. I read it, and then lent it about to all my acquaintance that had a sense for such things; from whom a similar verdict always came back. You say it is the first chapter of something greater. I call it rather the Foundation and Ground-plan on which you may build whatsoever of great and true has been given you to build. It is the true Apocalypse, this when the Open Secret becomes revealed to a man. I rejoice much in the glad serenity of soul with which you look out on this wondrous Dwelling-place of yours and mine,—with an ear for the *Ewigen Melodien*, which pipe in the winds round us, and utter themselves forth in all sounds and sights and things."

The difference between Carlyle and Emerson is the difference between the concrete and the abstract. Carlyle was interested in Men, Oliver, Frederick; Emerson was interested in Man. You cannot imagine Emerson writing a play or a novel, whereas Carlyle began his career by composing a novel, *Wotton Reinfred*, although he did not finish it. Carlyle wrote to him once, "I wish you would become *concrete*, and write in prose the straightest way." Emerson read few novels; one of the few he read was Scott's *Bride of Lammermoor*, and his good taste is shown by his enthusiasm for it. In Carlyle's *French Revolution*, the dead come to life again, and we see them in their habit as they lived. In Emerson's essays we sometimes move in a world of abstractions, breathing rarefied air.

The Correspondence of the two men—and they put the best that was in them into these letters— is one of the wise books of the world, like Boswell's *Life of Johnson* and Eckermann's *Conversations with Goethe*. It is a never-failing source of delight.

Emerson had a mind akin to that of Sir Thomas Browne, though he did not write like him. He loved hyperbole and mystery, but the richly deco-

rated Gothic style of the Norwich physician was
wholly unlike Emerson's disconnected simplicity.
It is difficult to read Emerson's prose in long
stretches, because of this structure.   As has been
well said, "the sentence is the unit."   In almost all
writing, the paragraph is the unit, and the mind
of the reader travels forward as easily as in a
chaise-and-four.   In Emerson it is difficult to see
the connexion between any sentence and those that
preceded or followed it.   I remember hearing Professor T. B. R. Briggs give a lecture on Pope, in
which he said that Dryden's couplets are like links
in a chain; Pope's are like pearls on a string.   Well,
that will do very well for Emerson's sentences.
Each phrase seems to have been worked over with
elaborate care.

Some one has wittily said that in Emerson's
Essays, "the whole is often less than the sum of its
parts."   This is a penetrating criticism.   We are
continually stimulated by a succession of epigrams—
but at the end, it is not always easy to state the
general purport.   It seems almost as if some of
his essays would read as well backwards as for-
wards; or one might begin in the middle and read
either way.   The important thing is that no matter
where you began, you would find something original
and striking, some sharp challenge to thought.

One reason for the lack of orderly sequence in
his compositions was owing to their conception and
parturition.   For most writers, there would be madness in this method.   Whenever a new idea struck
Emerson, which happened every few seconds, he

scribbled it down on whatever piece of paper lay within his reach; these scraps were all huddled together in some large receptacle.   When he sat down to compose, he plunged his hand into the mass, drew up a bunch, and then wrote his essay.   It was natural therefore that there should be some lack of connexion; but as a friend suggests, although the sentences were not always connected with one another, they were all connected with God.

His method of lecturing, astonishing as it may seem, was the same.   He came to the platform with a mass of papers in his hand, differing in colour, size, shape, and material.   Some were old envelopes, others receipted bills, others heavy wrapping paper.   The late Dr. Warren of Albany, told me that when he was about to graduate from Phillips Andover Academy, he wrote to Emerson, and asked him to deliver the Commencement address.   During the preliminary exercises, he sat beside the great man, who held in his hands the most motley collection of scraps of paper that could be imagined.   Finally he mounted the platform, and out of this heterogeneous mass of material gave an inspiring lecture.

The Rev. Dr. Albert O. White, of Orono, Maine, wrote me under date of 26 January 1917:

"When I heard Mr. Emerson read his lecture in the Divinity School of Harvard it was spoken of as his last public address.   He paused twice during the lecture to relieve the huskiness or maybe the feebleness of his voice, by some throat palliative which his daughter, who attended him, administered.   Dur-

ing those pauses, the audience conversed easily, and
gave eager and silent attention whenever Mr. Emerson arose from his seat to continue.   I recall viv-
idly that Mr. Emerson read from scraps of paper,
some of them manila wrapping paper, and the backs
of envelopes.   He read also from ordinary sheets
of writing paper."

Yet occasionally from this confusion came an
organic whole.   The essay on Napoleon, in *Representative Men,* is probably the most acute and the
wisest appraisal ever yet made.   It is surprising
that this Yankee farmer, who knew little of military
tactics and not much by experience of the world of
vehement action, should have estimated the character and genius of that soldier and statesman with
such accuracy.   It is uncanny.   He had no access to
archives, he knew not one-tenth of the facts that are
at the disposal of historians of today; yet his decision, handed down in 1850, will never be reversed.
After reading through the two fat volumes of the
Life of Napoleon by Holland Rose, I was interested
to see that his conclusion in all vital matters, was
that reached by Emerson.

From 1914 to 1919, I read Emerson's essay on
Napoleon through every year.   It was both stimulating and reassuring; it convinced me that where
Napoleon had failed, the Kaiser Wilhelm could not
succeed.   Both men wanted exactly the same thing;
the world.   It is not to be had by their methods,
for the Moral Law is as much a fact as the Law of
Gravitation.   Consider what Emerson says:

"Here was an experiment, under the most favorable conditions, of the powers of intellect without conscience. Never was such a leader so endowed, and so weaponed; never leader found such aids and followers. And what was the result of this vast talent and power, of these immense armies, burned cities, squandered treasures, immolated millions of men, of this demoralized Europe? It came to no result. All passed away, like the smoke of his artillery, and left no trace. He left France smaller, poorer, feebler, than he found it; and the whole contest for freedom was to be begun again. The attempt was, in principle, suicidal. France served him with life, and limb, and estate, as long as it could identify its interest with him; but when men saw that after victory was another war; after the destruction of armies, new conscriptions; and they who had toiled so desperately were never nearer to the reward,—they could not spend what they had earned, nor repose on their down-beds, nor strut in their châteaux,—they deserted him. Men found that his absorbing egotism was deadly to all other men. It resembled the torpedo, which inflicts a succession of shocks on any one who takes hold of it, producing spasms which contract the muscles of the hand, so that the man cannot open his fingers; and the animal inflicts new and more violent shocks, until he paralyzes and kills his victim. So, this exorbitant egotist narrowed, impoverished, and absorbed the power and existence of those who served him; and the universal cry of France, and of Europe, in 1814, was 'enough of him': 'assez de Bonaparte.'

"It was not Bonaparte's fault. He did all that in him lay, to live and thrive without moral principle. It was the nature of things, the eternal law of the man and the world, which balked and ruined him; and the result, in a million experiments would be the same. Every experiment, by multitudes or by individuals, that has a sensual and selfish aim, will fail. The pacific Fourier will be as inefficient as the pernicious Napoleon. As long as our civilization is essentially one of property, of fences, of exclusiveness, it will be mocked by delusions. Our riches will leave us sick; there will be bitterness in our laughter; and our wine will burn our mouth. Only that good profits, which we can taste with all doors open, and which serves all men."

Carlyle wrote to him of *Representative Men*:

"I found the Book a most finished clear and perfect set of *Engravings in the line manner;* portraitures full of *likeness,* and abounding in instruction and materials for reflection to me: thanks always for such a Book; and Heaven send us many more of them. *Plato,* I think, though it is the most admired by many, did least for me: little save Socrates with his clogs and big ears remains alive with me from it. *Swedenborg* is excellent in *likeness;* excellent in many respects;—yet I said to myself, on reaching your general conclusion about the man and his struggles: '*Missed* the consummate flower and divine elixir of Philosophy, say you? By Heaven, in clutching at it, and almost getting it, he has tumbled

into Bedlam,—which is a terrible *miss,* if it were
never so *near!*   A miss fully as good as a mile, I
should say!'—In fact, I generally dissented a little
about the *end* of all these Essays; which was notable, and not without instructive interest to me, as
I had so lustily shouted 'Hear, hear!' all the way
from the beginning up to that stage.—On the whole,
let us have another Book with your earliest con-
venience; that is the modest request one makes of
you on shutting this."

Although modern politics in Europe and in
America have taken exactly the opposite course to
that desired by Emerson the Individualist, his almost anarchistic utterances are weighty and perhaps in a higher state of civilisation may describe a
condition rather than a dream.   The difficulty is always with human nature.   An ideal government
would be absolute monarchy if the monarch were
all-wise and all-good; no such curiosities are to be
found.   An ideal government would also be absolute collectivism, if all the people were wise and
good; but that will never come to pass.   An ideal
government would also be absolute anarchy, where
every person did that which was right in his own
eyes, with no central authority, if every person were
wise and good; impossible.   Meanwhile, as under
any form of government, its success will depend
wholly on those who administer it, the best form
for an imperfect race in an imperfect world seems
to be representative democracy, with as much local
self-government as is possible.   For there is no

freedom except individual freedom, and no matter
how prosperous or mighty a nation may be, it is a
failure if the majority of its citizens are unhappy.
It is a myth to look beyond the individual. A business firm cannot be prosperous if both of its part-
ners are beggared by its policy.

Local self-government, the chief desideratum, has
vanished. When the Southern States of America
voted for the Federal income tax, they formally
killed and buried the doctrine of States Rights.
Everything tends everywhere toward centralisation;
the Federal Government has its clutch on every
man's private affairs and private opinions. There
are many who believe anything may be accomplished
by passing a federal law. We are now living in the
condition that Herbert Spencer predicted in his dying prophecy, *The Coming Slavery*.

Emerson was diametrically opposed to all this,
and his essay on Politics with its wisdom and
penetration, sounds in the twentieth century, like an
impossible dream.

"In dealing with the State, we ought to remember
that its institutions are not aboriginal, though they
existed before we were born: that they are not superior to the citizen: that every one of them was
once the act of a single man: that every law and
usage was a man's expedient to meet a particular
case: that they all are imitable, all alterable; we
may make as good; we may make better. Society
is an illusion to the young citizen. It lies before
him in rigid repose, with certain names, men, and

institutions, rooted like oak-trees to the centre, round which all arrange themselves the best they can.   But the old statesman knows that society is fluid; there are no such roots and centres; but any particle may suddenly become the centre of the movement and compel the system to gyrate round it, as every man of strong will, like Pisistratus, or Cromwell, or Paul, does forever.   But politics rest on necessary foundations, and cannot be treated with levity.   Republics abound in young civilians, who believe that the laws of the city, that grave modifications of the policy and modes of living, and employments of the population, that commerce, education, and religion, may be voted in or out; and that any measure, though it were absurd, may be imposed on a people, if only you can get sufficient voices to make it a law.   But the wise know that foolish legislation is a rope of sand, which perishes in the twisting; that the State must follow, and not lead, the character and progress of the citizen; the strongest usurper is quickly got rid of; and they only who build on Ideas, build for eternity; and that the form of government which prevails is the expression of what cultivation exists in the population which permits it.   The law is only a memorandum.   We are superstitious, and esteem the statute somewhat; so much life as it has in the character of living men, is its force.   The statute stands there to say, yesterday we agreed so and so, but how feel ye this article today?   Our statute is a currency, which we stamp with our own portrait: it soon becomes unrecogniz-

able, and in process of time will return to the mint.
Nature is not democratic, nor limited-monarchical,
but despotic, and will not be fooled or abated of any
jot of her authority, by the pertest of her sons; and
as fast as the public mind is opened to more intelligence, the code is seen to be brute and stammering.
It speaks not articulately, and must be made to.
Meantime the education of the general mind never
stops. The reveries of the true and simple are
prophetic. What the tender poetic youth dreams
and prays, and paints today, but shuns the ridicule
of saying aloud, shall presently be the resolutions
of public bodies, then shall be carried as grievance
and bill of rights through conflict and war, and then
shall be triumphant law and establishment for a
hundred years, until it gives place, in turn to new
prayers and pictures. The history of the State
sketches in coarse outline the progress of thought,
and follows at a distance the delicacy of culture and
of aspiration."

In his less inspired moments, Emerson's prose
style is often irritating. A mixture of dogma in
thought with vagueness of expression leads no-
whither. One feels that obvious obstacles are ig-
nored in such a philosophy and that the eyes of the
philosopher have lost the power of accommodation.
At such times he reminds us of those inhabitants of
Swift's Island of Laputa; each individual had two
eyes, but one looked inward and the other directly at
the zenith.

The works of Emerson, as they stand on my
shelves, fill eleven volumes, of which one contains
all the poems.   Yet if I had to choose, I had rather
keep the one volume of verse than the ten of prose.

His fragmentary, incoherent, disintegrated style,
which in his essays so often disturbs one's natural
feeling for continuity, is powerless to injure his
poems.   These are almost all short, separate pieces,
every one confined to the expression of only one
single mood or to the production of a single definite
effect.   He literally had no space to wander.   If
he had written long poems like *The Excursion,* or
Paracelsus, I dare say we should have had a repetition of the faults in the prose.

In his poems he is still more lofty, more thrill-
ingly intense.   There is an astonishing power of
concision.   There is no waste of energy.   He gives
us the quintessence of his thought, the last double-
distilled product of his observation and meditation.

Furthermore, Emerson's poetry appeals to me because it is so personal, intimate, confidential, confes-
sional: he tells us much of himself, and we never can
know too much.   When a poet, in addition to his
singing voice, has an interesting mind, his metrical
soliloquies compel attention.   Objective poems no
matter how beautiful, like Spenser's *Faery Queene*
and Tennyson's *Idylls of the King,* do not affect me
so deeply as Donne's lyrics, or Francis Thompson's
mystical musings.

Many of our chief American authors were ambi-
dextrous.   They wrote verse and prose with ap-
proximately equal skill.   Byron, Keats, Shelley,

Tennyson, Browning have no reputation as *prosa-
teurs;* whereas Poe, Holmes, Lowell and Emerson
are as distinguished in one field as in the other.
Emerson, unlike most poets, published his first volume of verse late in life; he was over forty years
old when his *Poems* appeared.   They express his
maturity of thought and vision.

He wrote to Carlyle,

"Long before this time you ought to have received from John Chapman a copy of *Emerson's
Poems,* so called, which he was directed to send you.
Poor man, you need not open them.   I know all
you can say.   I printed them, not because I was de-
ceived into a belief that they were poems, but because of the softness or hardness of heart of many
friends here who have made it a point to have them
circulated.   Once having set out to print, I obeyed
the solicitations of John Chapman, of an ill-omened
street in London, to send him the book in manuscript, for the better securing of copy-right.   In
printing them here I have corrected the most unpardonable negligences, which negligences must be all
stereotyped under his fair London covers and gilt
paper to the eyes of any curious London reader;
from which recollection I strive to turn away."

and received the following reply:

"I read your Book of Poems all faithfully, at
Bay House (our Hampshire quarters) ; where the
obstinate people,—with whom you are otherwise, in

prose, a first favourite,—foolishly *refused* to let me read aloud; foolishly, for I would have made it mostly all plain by commentary:—so I had to read for myself; and can say, in spite of my hard-heartedness, I did gain, though under impediments, a real satisfaction and some tone of the Eternal Melodies sounding, afar off, ever and anon, in my ear! This is fact; a truth in Natural History; from which you are welcome to draw inferences. A grand View of the Universe, everywhere the sound (unhappily *far off*, as it were) of a valiant, genuine Human Soul: this, even under rhyme, is a satisfaction worth some struggling for. But indeed you are very perverse; and through this perplexed *un*diaphanous element, you do not fall on me like radiant summer rainbows, like floods of sunlight, but with thin piercing radiances which affect me like the light of the *stars*."

Imagine a company of people refusing an offer to hear Carlyle read from Emerson's poems and comment upon them. Of all house-parties this one deserves the prize for stupidity. What do you suppose they did with the time saved by this dec-lination? Yet if their mental condition was so rudimentary that they did not care to hear Carlyle read Emerson, it is perhaps possible that they showed accurate self-judgment in refusing. Not even the combination of two men of genius could have pierced their social armour.

Carlyle was right in comparing Emerson's poetry to starlight. It lacks warmth, glow, colour, and

passion.   But there are times when a moonless sky
studded with stars is more beautiful than the Har-
vest Moon, and more significant than the sun at
noonday.

Edmund Clarence Stedman, usually so acute and
so just, made an unfortunate comparison when he
likened Emerson's style to that of Elizabethan dram-
atists.   No two kinds of poetry are more dissimilar.
Spontaneity and freshness of thought, easy, careless
grace of expression are the marks of the Eliza-
bethans.   Emerson resembles the generation who
followed the men of Elizabeth—the thinkers in
verse, the "Metaphysicals" who expressed curious
and original ideas in quaint oddities of metre.   He
is akin to the Sons of Donne, to Herbert, Vaughan,
Crashaw, Traherne, and Quarles.   He cared nothing for "smoothness," being more interested in the
rhythm of thought than in fluent melodies.

Without any intended disparagement of the reign-
ing poets of his time, Longfellow, Whittier,
Lowell, Poe, and Holmes, it is interesting to observe
how unaffected by them was Emerson.   He wrote
quite independently of tradition, expressing himself in his own way, so that the majority of his
readers thought that what he wrote was not poetry
at all, or that at all events he was no artist.

If we draw the old Latin distinction between
Vates and Poeta—between the Poet as Interpreter
and the Poet as Singer—we shall have to put Emerson in the former class.   If we divide poets into
those who stimulate our thoughts and those who
soothe our senses, or as Amy Lowell calls their

work respectively "Sword Blades and Poppy Seed," we shall once more have to place Emerson with the former group. He is closer to Donne than to Spenser; closer to Browning than to Tennyson; closer to the Seers than to the Bards. But our conception of poetry has widened so vastly since his day, partly owing to his influence, that what shocked his contemporaries is to us an agreeable tonic. Imagine what his readers must have thought of the first line of *Hamatreya*, which sounds like a city directory, and the third line, which sounds like a tariff schedule. Yet if they read on, they discovered that Emerson turned this unpromising material into poetry.

HAMATREYA

Bulkeley, Hunt, Willard, Hosmer, Merriam, Flint,
Possessed the land which rendered to their toil
Hay, corn, roots, hemp, flax, apples, wool and wood.
Each of these landlords walked amidst his farm,
Saying, " 'Tis mine, my children's and my name's.
How sweet the west wind sounds in my own trees!
How graceful climb those shadows on my hill!
I fancy these pure waters and the flags
Know me, as does my dog; we sympathize;
And, I affirm, my actions smack of the soil."
Where are these men? Asleep beneath their grounds
And strangers, fond as they, their furrows plough.
Earth laughs in flowers, to see her boastful boys
Earth-proud, proud of the earth which is not theirs;

Who steer the plough, but cannot steer their feet
Clear of the grave.

It is curious that this profound thinker, so given
to introspection and to universal contemplation,
should have been one of the foremost nature poets
of the nineteenth century; yet such is the fact.
This Sage, this oracular Prophet, was an accurate
and minute observer of natural objects.   Like the
wise man in the book of Proverbs, who learned
wisdom from birds, rabbits, and bugs, Emerson
studied with profit the titmouse, the squirrel, and
the bee.

In comparing his nature-poetry with that of
Bryant, we observe the difference between the tiny
and the vast, between the intimate and the general.
Bryant is all for large, simple effects; he loves a
winter landscape, the uneven expanse of ocean, the
unbroken forest, and the wide democracy of death.
Emerson is for the specific and the definite.   We
know how a snow-storm affected Bryant; this is
what it meant to Emerson.

THE SNOWSTORM

Announced by all the trumpets of the sky,
Arrives the snow, and, driving o'er the fields,
Seems nowhere to alight: the whited air
Hides hills and woods, the river, and the heaven,
And veils the farm-house at the garden's end.
The sled and traveller stopped, the courier's feet

Delayed, all friends shut out, the housemates sit
Around the radiant fireplace, enclosed
In a tumultuous privacy of storm.

Come see the north wind's masonry.
Out of an unseen quarry evermore
Furnished with tile, the fierce artificer
Curves his white bastions with projected roof
Round every windward stake, or tree, or door.
Speeding, the myriad-handed, his wild work
So fanciful, so savage, nought cares he
For number or proportion.   Mockingly,
On coop or kennel he hangs Parian wreaths;
A swan-like form invests the hidden thorn;
Fills up the farmer's lane from wall to wall,
Maugre the farmer's sighs; and at the gate
A tapering turret overtops the work.
And when his hours are numbered, and the world
Is all his own, retiring, as he were not,
Leaves, when the sun appears, astonished Art
To mimic in slow structures, stone by stone,
Built in an age, the mad wind's night-work,
The frolic architecture of the snow.

It is highly significant of Emerson's temperament
that in his masterpiece, *The Humble-Bee*, he should
have run exactly counter to traditional teaching.

> *How doth the little busy bee*
> *Improve each shining hour,*

did not appeal to him at all.   It was not the steady
toil of the bee, nor his high efficiency, that impressed

Emerson. It was rather the bee's philosophical tranquillity, delightful laziness, ability to take only what pleased him, and to make disaster absurd by sleeping through it. The bee does not toil too hard and he never worries at all. It is the deep wisdom of acquiescence.

Furthermore his first line employs an adjective that no one else would have thought of. Ordinarily, the last word we should use to describe an insect would be the word "burly." But how perfectly it fits the heavily-built, almost musclebound bumble bee!

THE HUMBLE-BEE

Burly, dozing humble-bee,
Where thou art is clime for me.
Let them sail for Porto Rique,
Far-off heats through seas to seek;
I will follow thee alone,
Thou animated torrid-zone!
Zigzag steerer, desert cheerer,
Let me chase thy waving lines;
Keep me nearer, me thy hearer,
Singing over shrubs and vines.

Insect lover of the sun,
Joy of thy dominion!
Sailor of the atmosphere;
Swimmer through the waves of air;
Voyager of light and noon;
Epicurean of June;

Wait, I prithee, till I come
Within earshot of thy hum,—
All without is martyrdom.

When the south wind, in May days,
With a net of shining haze
Silvers the horizon wall,
And with softness touching all,
Tints the human countenance
With a color of romance,
And infusing subtle heats,
Turns the sod to violets,
Thou, in sunny solitudes,
Rover of the underwoods,
The green silence dost displace
With thy mellow, breezy bass.

Hot midsummer's petted crone,
Sweet to me thy drowsy tone
Tells of countless sunny hours,
Long days, and solid banks of flowers;
Of gulfs of sweetness without bound
In Indian wildernesses found;
Of Syrian peace, immortal leisure,
Firmest cheer, and bird-like pleasure.

Aught unsavory or unclean
Hath my insect never seen;
But violets and bilberry bells,
Maple-sap and daffodels,
Grass with green flag half-mast high,
Succory to match the sky,

Columbine with horn of honey,
Scented fern and agrimony,
Clover, catch-fly, adder's-tongue
And briar-roses, dwelt among;
All beside was unknown waste,
All was picture as he passed.

Wiser far than human seer,
Yellow-breeched philosopher!
Seeing only what is fair,
Sipping only what is sweet,
Thou dost mock at fate and care,
Leave the chaff, and take the wheat.
When the fierce northwestern blast
Cools sea and land so far and fast,
Thou already slumberest deep;
Woe and want thou canst outsleep;
Want and woe, which torture us,
Thy sleep makes ridiculous.

The titmouse taught Emerson not merely inward contentment when outside storms are raging, but positive gayety of mind. It is not the Stoic "grin and bear it," who usually succeeds in doing neither, but the determination to turn the obstacle into a source of amusement, so that instead of crushing us, it actually ministers to our health and happiness. He was out walking in a blizzard, and became not only perplexed as to his path, but alarmed at the thought that he might be lost. Suddenly he saw a titmouse, a "scrap of valor," who was not only not troubled by the raging elements, but was literally having the time of his life, doing setting-up exercises in the snow.

In *The Mountain and the Squirrel*, he showed by a pleasantry the folly of all quantitative measurements; all things are equal in the divine scheme.

Not all of Emerson's poems are inspired, but there is only one that sounds insincere, only one that shows more pose than poise. That's the piece beginning

Goodbye, proud world, I'm going home,

which, as might be expected, was written in his youth. He recovered quickly from that adolescent cynicism.

The poem, *Two Rivers,* of which two stanzas should be quoted, illustrates his philosophy of thought, aroused by the contemplation of the quiet stream. Few poems anywhere show more beauty than the opening two lines:

TWO RIVERS

Thy summer voice, Musketaquit,
Repeats the music of the rain;
But sweeter rivers pulsing flit
Through thee, as thou through Concord Plain.

Thou in thy narrow banks art pent:
The stream I love unbounded goes
Through flood and sea and firmament;
Through light, through life, it forward flows.

Essential to an understanding of his thought is *The Problem,* two lines from which are on his tomb. This expresses fittingly his idea of the Over-Soul, the Divine Flux; that men are more passive than active, and men of genius most passive of all, being open to the Divine Influence. It is perhaps strange that this philosophical doctrine of Passivity should be held so tenaciously by one who was forever calling upon man to be independent, active, alert, and progressive. But it is vain to hope for consistency in any philosophy or in any philosopher.

Emerson's own favourite among his poems is *Daughters of Time.* An author's choice is always interesting, and seldom ratified by his readers. I would not exchange *The Humble-Bee* for a hundred *Daughters of Time.*

Although Emerson was an ardent American, and called upon America to have a scholarship and a philosophy of her own, his influence is steadily widening in Europe and in Asia. Maeterlinck has been profoundly affected by him, and contributed an essay upon him as an Introduction to a French translation. German works on Emerson have multiplied rapidly, and it is curious to see how strong an effect he had upon Nietzsche, whose Superman is a sinister reproduction of the Emersonian hero, a kind of devil's portrait.

Apart from the thrilling beauty of isolated passages in Emerson's verse and prose, it is his spiritual leadership that has placed him among the Lights of the world. Who cares whether Arnold was right or wrong in his famous lecture? What difference does it make whether Emerson was a great writer or a great man who wrote?   He inspires us under either classification.   We love and honour him for what he has taught us, and his teaching has sunk so deeply into humanity that if every one of his books should be destroyed, his influence would go on its fructifying course through many generations. We have taken in Emerson with our mothers' milk. He has had a profounder effect on humanity than on schools of thought; he has more deeply affected individual lives than literary art.

Mr. Woodberry says, "His is the only great mind that America has produced in literature."   This is a hard saying, and one that was probably meant to be a challenge.   But it is certain that his works expressed only a part of his mighty personality.   He saw and felt things that could not be written.

Mr. Woodberry also says, "He is the priest of those who have gone out of the church."   Well, I have not gone out of the church, nor shall I until I am convinced that I am greater than the church. Why not rather call Emerson the great Ally of the church?   He was surely not far from the kingdom of God.   The best thing Matthew Arnold said of him was this: *he is the friend of all those who would live in the spirit.*

VI

THE AMERICAN HUMORIST
MARK TWAIN

WHEN I was a schoolboy in Hartford, I frequently saw Mark Twain on the street. He was so conspicuous that the jest of G. K. Chesterton will apply perfectly. Some admirer said to the Englishman, "It must be wonderful just to take a walk and have everybody know who you are." "Yes," replied Chesterton, "and if they don't know, they ask." The Englishman had been made noticeable by nature; the American by his own deliberate intention. Apparently he never had his hair cut; it fell in dark masses around his neck, and received his daily personal attention; in cold weather he wore a short coat of sealskin, with the fur side outside; in walking, he rolled widely to right and left, in the manner of a sailor in musical comedy. He was distinguishable one hundred yards away, and people who happened to turn around, waited for him to pass, then remained as if hypnotised, staring after his slowly diminishing figure. Those who had seen him before found him well worth seeing again; those who had never seen him asked the nearest by-stander who he was, and their already awakened curiosity received a tremendous lift by the answer.

He was too much of a humorist to be conceited.

He was not conceited at all, nor was there anything about him unattractive. Howells, who disliked even the reminiscent odour of tobacco, loved to be in the company of Mark, who was a pillar of cloud by day, and an intermittent flashlight by night. Even Mark's profanity was lyrical rather than vulgar. When he became engaged to Olivia Langdon —curious assonance, his mother's name was Lambton, his middle name was Langhorne, and he married a Langdon—he knew that the engagement might be broken if she once heard him swear. By superhuman efforts he made his speech, Yea, Yea, and Nay, Nay, and for some time after the wedding, his language was so austere that she did not dream of his oral efficiency. But one day, thinking he was alone (perhaps even Emerson swore when he was alone) he tried to make the new telephone work, with the usual result. (The Paris *Figaro* says that to get your telephone connexion is not an achievement; it is a career.) Mark found it particularly exasperating on this occasion, and suddenly shot out a veritable Missouri barrage. Then "looking up, aware he somehow grew" of the presence of his wife, who regarded him with the same incredulous amazement as she would have listened to a similar outburst from the preacher in church. Having read somewhere that the way to cure your husband of swearing is to swear yourself, she said in a dull, toneless voice, *Blankety-Blank-Blank*. To which Mark replied, "Oh, darling, you know the words, but you don't know the tune!"

He loved to be conspicuous, and saw no reason—
and indeed there was none—why he should not
gratify this desire. Late in life, his magnificent
hair turned white, and he wore garments to match,
appearing in Washington drawing-rooms in evening-
clothes the colour of snow. I think that this dis-
regard of averages and love of dramatic display
were partly caused by his fierce independence. His
hatred of literary conventions which made him write
travel-books and boys' books unlike the accepted
manner, made him dress as pleased his fancy rathei
than in accordance with the mode. Perhaps independence in clothes takes more courage than independence in opinions; he had courage enough for
both, with a plentiful supply left over foi an emer
gency.

He was in his way as prominent in a crowd as
Daniel Webster. Everybody stopped to look at
him, and indeed he was worth looking at, his leonine
face expressing, as every one knew, his lion-heart.
When he received in 1907 the Doctor's degree from
the University of Oxford—which he regarded as
the highest honour of his life—in the eyes of the
crowd he stood alone, though in fact he was accompanied by Rudyard Kipling, General William Booth,
the famous astronomer Ball, and two distinguished
Frenchmen. In the procession outdoors and on
the platform within, nobody saw any one else. I
was reading shortly afterwards a French periodical,
which said that of course France was honoured by
the bestowal of two degrees on her native sons; but

that it would be futile to say that these two or any other guest received notice in any way comparable to that given to Mark Twain.   This expedition to England which reached its climax at Oxford was such as perhaps no other American author has ever experienced.   All classes of society united in doing homage.   It must have been a happy moment for him when he walked down the gangplank of the steamer and the stevedores on the dock gave him cheers of welcome.   Upon his departure the universal emotion reached such a sensational climax that a London newspaper said, "No foreigner has ever been treated as he has been by the English people. . . . The highest and the greatest in the land have joined eagerly in all forms of tribute to this untitled friend of all mankind. . . . If the truth must be told, Twain's popularity in England is of a warmer and more personal nature than even in his own country.   He has won the hearts of Englishmen as no living writer has done, and they love to do him honour."   Again: "Of all the American men of letters, Twain may safely be said to have had the warmest appreciation in the British Isles . . . the sterling worth and deathless character underlying the topmost froth of thought in the humorist makes the entire nation grapple him to their hearts with hoops of steel."

How amazed the young obscure Kipling and the American who was regarded only as a joker, would have been, as they sat talking together one hot afternoon in Elmira, could they have known that the day would come when they would stand together and receive academic honours from the University of Oxford!

The story of his life is adequately given by A. B. Paine, in the three-volume biography, perhaps the finest biographical work ever written in America. It is as interesting as any of Mark Twain's own writings, because the biographer with a self-efface-ment as unusual as it is admirable, has kept his hero ever before the reader's eyes. We see him; we hear him talk; we know him. And it is clear, that although he was a painstaking literary artist, his genius was spontaneous. There are hundreds of his sayings and acts that came from direct inspiration. The story of his life, from his childhood in a Mis-souri river-town to that great day at Oxford, is more romantic than romance itself. And the final astounding elevation was caused simply by the pos-session of genius, from which he did his utmost to escape, but which would not be denied. Had the Mississippi not been closed to navigation, he would have remained as pilot in absolute contentment; was not the pilot king of the river? Had he and his partner not missed wealth in a mine by a few min-utes he would never have written a book; does not money fulfill the heart's desire?

As we look back, it seems strange that his world-wide fame did not come to him till he was an old man; all the stranger because the books on which his fame securely rests were not only written before he was fifty, but attained an enormous popularity.

The Innocents Abroad was published when he was thirty-four; *Roughing It* when he was thirty-six; *The Adventures of Tom Sawyer* when he was forty-one; *Life on the Mississippi* when he was forty-seven; *Huckleberry Finn* when he was forty-nine. Yet the critics apparently took neither him nor his art seriously, nor conceded him any place in literature. And there he stood, incomparably the greatest living American novelist, whose books, instead of being neglected, were the delight of every American home! It is the simple truth to say that instead of being discovered by the critics and historians, he was forced upon their attention by universal suffrage. A man of the people, he owed to their adoration his final renown.

It was the sweeter when it came. At the seventieth birthday celebration in New York, it was clear that all the Americans who attended or sent letters looked upon him as their chief. The guests were exclusively composed of creative writers, and they numbered one hundred and seventy. In the midst of the festivities, a cablegram came from England with the signatures of forty English authors, among them being George Meredith, Thomas Hardy, Rudyard Kipling, Arthur Balfour, Anthony Hope, and Conan Doyle.

Why did prodigious popularity so long precede fame? There are authors who have a vast public and never will have any reputation; and there are those of enviable fame—like Henry James—who perhaps never will have many readers. Here the

case is different. Two reasons may partly account
for it.

His books were so original that although received
with rapture, they were too strange for classification,
which is the curse of criticism. His *Innocents
Abroad* was quite unlike any other book that had
preceded it, whilst *Tom Sawyer* and *Huckleberry
Finn* were stories about boys that had all the queer
shock of truth. Never was there a great writer
who owed less to literature and to accepted art.

Again, there is no doubt that his power to make
men laugh had a crippling effect on his literary
standing. Had Shakespeare first attained popularity by the creation of Falstaff many honest souls
would have eagerly tried to "see the joke" in Ham-
let, which has since been abundantly supplied by the
commentators. Mark Twain was both serious and
sentimental; and no one knows what he suffered
when his seriousness was taken as mockery and his
sentiment as burlesque. He was once asked to
deliver an address at a girls' college, and he unfortunately decided that they would appreciate an
original thoughtful poem. When he appeared on
the platform, he was greeted with shrieks of pro-
leptic laughter; he had to wait until they calmed
down. Then he said solemnly, "I have written an
original poem," at which there was enormous merri-
ment. "I mean it," he said sternly, which magnified
the mirth. He felt in his pocket, took out the manuscript, and said, "Here it is." This was received
with hysterical delight. Then he saw that to read

it was impossible, and he remarked, "After all, I won't read it," which put the room into convulsions. The girls decided that never had a humorist begun an address more happily. What would they have thought if they could have listened to the torrent of blasphemy that he released on his way home!

I remember very well as a boy the disagreeable shock caused by the appearance of *The Prince and the Pauper.* The disgusted verdict was, "It isn't funny," and I heard more than one person express regret that Mark Twain should have thought himself capable of writing a novel. "Does he imagine that he is a real author?"

American humour is not always understood by foreigners. Paul Heyse told me that he had read every word of *Huckleberry Finn,* and had not laughed once, which is almost as funny as anything in the book. I suppose that one reason why many ill-informed Americans say that Englishmen have no sense of humour, is because the English do not indulge so commonly as we in boisterous jocularity, exaggeration, surprise, and broad burlesque. The average Englishman does not see why a stranger should accost him with jocosity—many Englishmen do not see why a stranger should accost them at all. In an American city on a terrifically hot day, two hitherto unacquainted gentlemen will speak to each other, one saying, "Don't you wish you had brought your overcoat?" which small change is returned by the other with equal affability. If you said that to an Englishman, he would look at you blankly, and finally ask, "You mean of course your *light* over-

coat?" Meeting a resident Englishman at a hotel
luncheon in Vancouver, I remarked gently, "Of
course you are way behind the times here in Vancouver, but I shouldn't think you would be so bla-
tant about it." "What on earth do you mean?"
he enquired. Then I called his attention to the
meal card, on which was printed, *Vancouver, B. C.*
"But it doesn't mean *that*, you know," he exclaimed,
trying to set me right. I don't think he was de-
ficient in humour; I was a stranger, and therefore
not sufficiently intimate to be taken otherwise than
seriously.

Now *Punch* is the first of all comic papers, and the
English abound in humour of their own kind. No
less a personage than Woodrow Wilson told me a
story which shows how dangerous it is to assume
that your intended victim has no sense of humour.
Three Americans were lamenting the fact that the
English were without humour, when they saw a
representative of that nation approaching, and it
was agreed that he should be tested. So one of the
three stopped him and told him a side-splitting yarn.
The Englishman received the climax with a face of
leather. The American, somewhat nettled, cried
"You'll laugh at that next summer." "No," said
the Englishman gravely, "I think not." "Why
not?" "Because I laughed at that *last* summer."

Typical American humour is not subtle, per-
vasive, or ironical; it is made up largely of bur-
lesques, exaggerations, and surprises—of all three
Artemus Ward and Mark Twain were accomplished
masters. Mark Twain's books of travel, his essays,

and the episodes and soliloquies he introduced into his novels, afford abundant illustrations. Then there is a peculiar humour all his own, which no one else could either have imagined or expressed. This, which is perhaps his best vein, comes out in earnest conversations between two persons arguing at cross purposes. The dialogue on the French language between Huck and Jim is unsurpassable.

"Why, Huck, doan' de French people talk de same way we does?"

"No, Jim; you couldn't understand a word they said—not a single word."

"Well, now, I be ding-busted! How do dat come?"

"*I* don't know; but it's so. I got some of their jabber out of a book. S'pose a man was to come to you and say Polly-voo-franzy—what would you think?"

"I wouldn' think nuff'n; I'd take en bust him over de head—dat is, if he warn't white. I wouldn't 'low no nigger to call me dat."

"Shucks, it ain't calling you anything. It's only saying, do you know how to talk French?"

"Well, den, why couldn't he *say* it?"

"Why, he *is* a-saying it. That's a Frenchman's *way* of saying it."

"Well, it's a blame' ridicklous way, en I doan' want to hear no mo' 'bout it. Dey ain' no sense in it."

"Looky here, Jim; does a cat talk like we do?"

"No, a cat don't."

"Well, does a cow?"

"No, a cow don't, nuther."

"Does a cat talk like a cow, or a cow talk like a cat?"

"No, dey don't."

"It's natural and right for 'em to talk different from each other, ain't it?"

"Course."

"And ain't it natural and right for a cat and a cow to talk different from *us?*"

"Why, mos' shoiy it is."

"Well, then, why ain't it natural and right for a *Frenchman* to talk different from us? You answer me that."

"Is a cat a man, Huck?"

"No."

"Well, den, dey ain't no sense in a cat talkin' like a man. Is a cow a man?—er is a cow a cat?"

"No, she ain't either of them."

"Well, den, she ain't got no business to talk like either one er the yuther of 'em. Is a Frenchman a man?"

"Yes."

"*Well*, den! Dad blame it, why doan he *talk* like a man? You answer me *dat!*"

I see it warn't no use wasting words—you can't learn a nigger to argue. So I quit.

Lieut. Merrit Heminway, of Watertown, Connecticut, who commanded a company of coloured troops in France during the World War, tells me that when some of his men went up to the French coloured auxiliaries, the latter asked them the same question that Jim resented—*Parlez-vous français?* This well-meant interrogation was answered by blows from the Americans, who could not believe that their foreign black brethren were not making fun of them. Not for an instant could the Americans grasp the fact that every negro did not talk English.

A sense of humour is almost invariably accompanied by common sense, and there can be too much of both. Common sense and a sense of humour save a man from making himself ridiculous, but they often keep him from making himself anything else. Just as a stream of water will disperse a mob more effectively than bullets, so many men lose their courage and their convictions in the face of ridicule. The great leaders of thought, the great mystics, have not always been conspicuous for their humour, and they triumphed over the last fear—the fear of being laughed at. The only first-rate philosopher who abounded in humour was Schopenhauer—and he was a pessimist. There is a remarkable passage in Compton Mackenzie's novel, *The Altar Steps,* where the young ritualist is writing to his rector: "One hears of the saving grace of humour, but I'm not sure that humour is a saving grace. I rather wish that I had no sense of humour. It's a destructive quality. All the great sceptics have been humorists. Humour is really a device to secure human comfort. Take me. I am inspired to become a preaching friar. I instantly perceive the funny side of setting out to be a preaching friar. I tell

myself that other people will perceive the funny side
of it, and that consequently I shall do no good as a
preaching friar. Yes, humour is a moisture which
rusts everything except gold."

This is a profound saying. I believe that Mark
Twain's inordinate sense of humour partly explains
his incapacity to appreciate certain masterpieces of
art, and his inability to believe in religion. Common sense and fun are good guides in practical emergencies and on low levels; but they are an actual
hindrance often to interpretation and to spiritual
progress. Mark Twain's book on Shakespeare was
appalling in the ignorance it displayed; and with no
guide to religion except humour and common sense,
it is not surprising that he saw just nothing. His
absolute pessimism, like that of many humorists, was
the mind defeating itself. He regarded death as
more fortunate than birth, and life as a bad practical
joke played on man by destiny. Like most non-reli-
gious men, he fortunately failed to live up to his
creed. Christians, with all their failures, are as a
rule more consistent than non-Christians. Mark
Twain ridiculed self-sacrifice, and altruism, but his
daily life was full of acts of unselfish kindness.
The men that he most admired and liked to have
near him were W. D. Howells, a veritable child of
God, and Joseph Twichell, a devout minister of the
Gospel.

Mark Twain was like Jonathan Swift. He hated
and despised *that animal called man,* but he loved
with all his heart Tom, Dick, and Harry. When
he read the daily papers, he snorted with rage at

human folly and meanness; but he had a positive
genius for friendship.

The key to his intellectual attitude in social and
political relations is the word Democracy. He was
the great American Democrat. Indeed in literature
he is the representative American, as in politics was
Abraham Lincoln. Nothing enraged him more
than snobbery, artificial distinctions, cruelty, and
injustice. There was forever in him the Eternal
Boy, and nothing rankles in a boy's mind more than
unfairness. If only parents and teachers could remember that fact!

One reason why he ridiculed all conceptions of
Heaven was doubtless because Heaven seemed to
him undemocratic.

All the Philistines in America became articulate
in Mark Twain. His *Connecticut Yankee in King
Arthur's Court,* which has been condemned as destructive to all fine feelings, and which is certainly
marred by grotesque faults, is a roaring expression
of his democratic creed. Yet, like most humorists,
Mark Twain was not in the least a political radical.
The notion of socialism was hateful to him, he believed with all his might in personal property, he
was quite unjust to French literature because he
thought it immoral, and his belief in the sacredness
of marriage was so staunch that Gorki never recovered from Mark's practical demonstration of it.

Humour is a conservative force; from Aris-
tophanes to Mark Twain it has been the weapon of
conservative writers. Radicals often lack humour.
But above all, Mark Twain was a literary artist,

a great writer. I have no sympathy with those who either at the time or later felt shocked at his failure to impress Emerson, Holmes, Longfellow and others at the famous Boston dinner. The Olympians themselves may be pardoned for not appreciating him, for hardly any one in America realised his true position. As a literary artist there was no man in the room his superior. Instead of being an uncouth joker admitted by sufferance to the society of the elect, and expected to show due reverence, he was sitting with them as a peer.

It is impossible to compare *The Scarlet Letter* with *Huckleberry Finn.* But this may be said; of all the novels written by Americans, these two stand out conspicuously above the rest. The delicate, fastidious, impeccable art of one is matched by the prodigious vitality and truth of the other. It is like the impossible comparison of Turgenev and Tolstoi. The former was incomparably the finer and more subtle artist; the latter was Life itself.

As an interpreter of American life, Mark Twain's fame rests on five books; two of them historical, three of them creative fiction. I refer of course to *Roughing It, Life on the Mississippi, Tom Sawyer, Huckleberry Finn,* and *Pudd'nhead Wilson.*

With the same means of locomotion employed by Jehu, Julius Cæsar, and other worthies, Mark Twain travelled from the Mississippi River to the Pacific Coast; and his book *Roughing It* gives a picture of that vast country in the sixties that no other writer has equalled. Every American interested in the growth of his native land should read and reread this book; amid all the anecdotes, the jokes, and the exaggerations, the Truth is there. Such was life in Nevada, such was life in California; such were the people and such were their actions. In his preface, Mark professed to give merely a personal narrative of a vagabond adventure; but he knew that he was able to furnish first-hand information, and he combined his history with a prophecy and with an irrepressible burst of fun.

"Still, there is information in the volume; information concerning an interesting episode in the history of the Far West, about which no books have been written by persons who were on the ground in person, and saw the happenings of the time with their own eyes. I allude to the rise, growth, and culmination of the silver-mining fever in Nevada— a curious episode, in some respects; the only one, of its peculiar kind, that has occurred in the land; and the only one, indeed, that is likely to occur in it. "Yes, take it all around, there is quite a good deal of information in the book. I regret this very much, but really it could not be helped: information appears to stew out of me naturally, like the precious ottar of roses out of the otter."

In addition to his vivid pictures of life in California, he wrote, in the concluding chapters of the book, the finest and most picturesque account of the Hawaiian Islands that I have read anywhere.

Perhaps the best and the worst of Mark Twain may be found in the two volumes called *Life on the*

THE AMERICAN HUMORIST 179

Mississippi. The first half of that work is epical
in its magnificent sweep of vision; his descriptions
of the various aspects of the mighty river at all
hours of the day and night are worthy of any pen
in history; the second volume reads like the ephemeral stuff turned out by any hack to accompany a
railway timetable or a hotel circular. After he left
St. Louis and started north, leaving the scenes of
his youth, his inspiration deserted him, and he became statistical and impossible. But in sheer
literary art, the first volume of the Mississippi-book
contains the finest examples of his mastery of the
English language. One might almost say that nobody ever described anything anywhere in a more
vivid manner.

Is there any other instance in history where an
individual is more closely identified with a river?
It is impossible to see the mighty Mississippi or to
hear its name without thinking of Mark Twain.
How unfortunate it is that the passenger steamers
run no longer between its banks! There are enough
tourists all over the world, one would think, who are
so familiar with Mark Twain and with what he has
written about the Mississippi, to make it feasible to
furnish them the opportunity to take this literary
pilgrimage, from St. Louis to New Orleans. I can
see in imagination passengers crowding the decks,
with copies of Mark Twain's books in their hands,
identifying the places. For my own part, one of
the unsatisfied ambitions of my life is to take the
whole journey by water, from St. Paul to the Gulf
Perhaps I shall manage this some day.

Some years ago, being in Carbondale in southern Illinois on a day in Spring, I enquired of a resident, "How far is it to the Mississippi?" I was informed it was seventeen miles. That afternoon, we journeyed thither in a Ford car. I had seen the Mississippi at St. Paul, at St. Louis, at Memphis, at New Orleans; but I wanted to see it in its naked majesty, rolling away through the country, uncontaminated by city filth. I saw it. There was no town in sight, not even a building on its banks. Far as the eye could reach, the splendid river dominated the view. Away to the North, it came sweeping around a wooded bend, and the trees on the Missouri side were in living green; away to the South, it lost itself in the misty distance. One mile wide, forty feet deep, and running seven miles an hour, "too full for sound and foam," it swept by in silent majesty. I could almost imagine a steamer passing, with Mark Twain at the wheel; and I saw even more clearly than with the physical eye, the old raft floating along, with Huck and Jim engaged in argumentative conversation.

Every great river has a personality; Mark Twain has made all his readers feel the individuality, character, and temperament of the Mississippi. So long as it flows, so long will his name be identified with it.

Huckleberry Finn is a greater book than *Tom Sawyer,* because with the same realism, the same humour, the same sharp characterisation, it is the work of one who was at heart a poet. Tom is the "smart" American boy, sophisticated, prudent, assertive, bossy; as a man, he will exhibit a genius for administration, and will be a great executive, a captain of industry, or the president of some well-tentacled corporation. Huck is the child of nature, unspoiled, with that vivid, pictorial imagination that so often characterises men who can neither read nor write. A clever modern journalist might have conceived the boy Tom, and made him live; but only a literary genius could have created Huck. And as for Jim, if there has ever been a reader who did not love Jim, we may be sure he could not love anybody or anything. The beautiful and the tragic aspects of slavery are embodied in that personification of loyalty.

Pudd'nhead Wilson is remarkable not only for the story, but for the aphorisms at the chapter-heads. For keen worldly wisdom, for knowledge of life and humanity on the earthly side, these are as profound as mundane philosophy can be. There is another virtue in this book; it is a valuable contribution to the social history of slavery in the United States. As I have said elsewhere, Mark Twain is the most truthful and the most reliable of all novelists who have dealt with American slavery. Mrs. Stowe did not give a faithful picture of slavery; she gave a faithful picture of Abolition sentiment. If one wishes to know what slavery actually was, *Uncle Tom's Cabin* would not be the most reliable authority, not any authority at all; but if one wishes to know exactly what the Northern Abolitionists thought about slavery, the burning intensity of their sincere convictions, Mrs. Stowe's book is an imperishable and accurate witness. On the other hand

the stories of Thomas Nelson Page and Hopkinson
Smith are not true pictures of slavery as an institution; for they, like Mrs. Stowe, (only on the other
side) wrote propaganda; they represented the
charming, patriarchal element in the "Sacred Institution," as they knew and remembered it. They
were not witnesses; they were advocates. But
Mark Twain, with no propaganda, seeing life with
the clear eye of the humorist, gave us both comedy
and tragedy; in one picture in *Pudd'nhead Wilson*
he would convince any one who needed convincing
that slavery had to be abolished. I refer to that
moment when the poor, ignorant, deluded negress,
who had, like all her race, an unspeakable horror of
being sold "down the river," and who had spent the
night on board the boat in the dream of going
northward, sees in the revealing dawn that horrible
snag, with the water swirling around it, and wakes
to tragic actuality. Had that book been written
before 1860, it would have been worth a hundred
speeches by Phillips and Garrison.

In Mark Twain's attacks and defences—for he
was often irresistibly impelled to attack or to defend
somebody or something—one feels the severity of
his artistic and moral standards. He was one of
the most painstaking writers known to fame; every
word was carefully chosen, his punctuation was religious in its intensity, and he used *italic type* with the
utmost care. All of his sentences were written to
be read aloud; and those of us who heard him often
on the platform, can hear his voice now on the
printed page. He was an enthusiastic admirer of

Browning; he used to say that he could make any poem in Browning clear by reading it aloud, and his own copy of the poet's works is filled with underlined and doubly-underlined words, which he stressed in interpretation. We know how careful he was of his dialect in all his novels; and the study of his italics is enlightening. It was because he took such pains in writing that he despised the works of Scott and Cooper, and failed to do justice to the merits of those Romantics; he could not forgive them for their impromptu books; for the slovenly haste in composition which Mark thought traitorous to art. On the other hand, he was filled with a romantic chivalry all his own, that made him spring to the defence of Harriet Shelley and Joan of Arc; he might ridicule the Catholic religion, but in his own heart he had canonised Joan long before she received the Papal sanction. His work on Joan of Arc, which for a time he was mistaken enough to think his master-piece, had its origin in a kind of romantic chivalry. He, who believed nothing, exalted the Inspired Maid, who believed everything.

Likewise, when a sensationalist who called him-self Max O'Rell attacked America, Mark Twain held up the little plaintiff so that all the world could see him, and then buried him under an ava-lanche of boisterous mirth. But perhaps he never enjoyed defending or attacking anything so much as when he defended the English style of General Grant against an attack from Matthew Arnold. Grant was one of Mark's heroes; he could not bear to see him criticised; but when the adverse critic was Mat-

thew Arnold, who, in Mark's mind was the very
Image of all Snobs, and when the Englishman's
attack was directed against General Grant's *grammar,* could there be a more inviting opportunity?
Our American took up the Challenge joyfully, and in
a speech which drew universal attention, defended
the dead soldier.

"People may hunt out what microscopic motes
they please, but after all, the fact remains and cannot be dislodged, that General Grant's book is a
great, and in its peculiar department, unique, and
unapproachable literary masterpiece.   In their line,
there is no higher literature than those modest,
simple memoirs.   Their style is at least flawless
and no man could improve upon it, and great books
are weighed and measured by their style and matter,
and not by the trimmings and shadings of their
grammar.

"There is that about the sun which makes us for-
gets his spots and when we think of General Grant
our pulses quicken and his grammar vanishes; we
only remember that this is the simple soldier, who
all untaught of the silken phrase-makers, linked
words together with an art surpassing the art of
the schools and put into them a something which
will still bring to American ears, as long as America
shall last, the roll of his vanished drums and the
tread of his marching hosts.   What do we care
for grammar when we think of those thunderous
phrases,—'unconditional and immediate surrender,'
'I propose to move immediately upon your works,'

'I propose to fight it out on this line if it takes all summer.' Mr. Arnold would doubtless claim that that last phrase is not strictly grammatical, and yet it did certainly wake up this Nation as a hundred million tons of A. No. 1, fourth-proof, hardboiled, hide-bound grammar, from another mouth could not have done. And finally we have that gentler phrase, that one which shows you another true side of the man, shows you that in his soldier heart there was room for other than gory war mottoes and in his tongue the gift to fitly phrase them:—'let us have peace.' "

Mark Twain had, in common with all great humorists, a tremendous capacity for Indignation. Those who had the privilege of hearing him talk when some particular manifestation of cruelty, or stupidity, or snobbery supplied the necessary spark, know something of his denunciatory fluency. And it is my conviction that Indignation was a fundamental quality in his whole intellectual attitude. His philosophy of democracy was largely inspired by this emotion; and his uncompromising pessimism was built on it. Such a book as *The Mysterious Stranger* sprang directly from it. The chronic folly of mankind infuriated him; and he hated also the Idea of God, as it appeared in orthodox religious thought; for if God were really responsible for such a world as Mark believed this to be, He ought to be treated like any other capricious and cold-hearted tyrant. It is perhaps strange, when so many humble individuals who lack health, money, and fame face their fate with uncomplaining cheerfulness, that Mark Twain, who enjoyed everything that life can give, material comfort, foreign travel, family love, and the adoration of the world, should have regarded the universe with such implacable hostility.

But as he never made any important contribution to philosophical thought, his *naif* meditations will be forgotten; his works of literary art cannot be forgotten, for they have in them the very principle of life.

Possibly one cannot be a great humorist without having an overwhelming sense of the woe of the world, and without an overpowering desire to lessen it. I found in a German periodical, *Die schöne Literatur,* a short article on Mark Twain that would have pleased him. The anonymous critic wrote, "Although Mark Twain's humour arouses irresistible laughter, his main object is not reached through that, for in his case, like that of all other genuine humorists, Wit is united with Sorrow (*Weltschmerz*) ; he has as his true goal something higher and nobler, the determination to bring to the attention of mankind evil customs and alterable obstacles, in order that human beings may become better and nobler."

Underneath Mark Twain's mirth there is undoubtedly this fierce passion for Improvement— perhaps he would in the last analysis have defined it as an intense desire for Fair Play. This brings us back to the point where all discussions of Mark Twain's religion must begin and end—he was a Democrat. He was the incarnate spirit of America,

and it is our fault that he represented the ideals of
America rather than what actually prevails. Yet
we are, with all our shortcomings and perversities
and inconsistencies and sins, an idealistic nation;
and in him we found a Voice.